DISEASES AND DISORDERS

MAJOR DEPRESSIVE DISORDER

By Simon Pierce

Portions of this book originally appeared in *Depression* by Lydia Bjornlund.

LUCENT
PRESS

Published in 2018 by
Lucent Press, an Imprint of Greenhaven Publishing LLC
353 3rd Avenue
Suite 255
New York, NY 10010

Designer: Andrea Davison-Bartolotta
Editor: Jennifer Lombardo

Cataloging-in-Publication Data

Names: Pierce, Simon.
Title: Major depressive disorder / Simon Pierce.
Description: New York : Lucent Press, 2018. | Series: Diseases and disorders | Includes index.
Identifiers: ISBN 9781534561236 (library bound) | ISBN 9781534561243 (ebook)
Subjects: LCSH: Depression, Mental–Juvenile literature. | Depression in children–Juvenile literature. | Psychology–Juvenile literature.
Classification: LCC RC537.P54 2018 | DDC 618.92'8527–dc23

Printed in the United States of America

CPSIA compliance information: Batch #BS17KL: For further information contact Greenhaven Publishing LLC, New York, New York at 1-844-317-7404.

Please visit our website, www.greenhavenpublishing.com. For a free color catalog of all our high-quality books, call toll free 1-844-317-7404 or fax 1-844-317-7405.

CONTENTS

FOREWORD

Illness is an unfortunate part of life, and it is one that is often misunderstood. Thanks to advances in science and technology, people have been aware for many years that diseases such as the flu, pneumonia, and chicken pox are caused by viruses and bacteria. These diseases all cause physical symptoms that people can see and understand, and many people have dealt with these diseases themselves. However, sometimes diseases that were previously unknown in most of the world turn into epidemics and spread across the globe. Without an awareness of the method by which these diseases are spread—through the air, through human waste or fluids, through sexual contact, or by some other method—people cannot take the proper precautions to prevent further contamination. Panic often accompanies epidemics as a result of this lack of knowledge.

Knowledge is power in the case of mental disorders, as well. Mental disorders are just as common as physical disorders, but due to a lack of awareness among the general public, they are often stigmatized. Scientists have studied them for years and have found that they are generally caused by hormonal imbalances in the brain, but they have not yet determined with certainty what causes those imbalances or how to fix them. Because even mild mental illness is stigmatized in Western society, many people prefer not to talk about it.

Chronic pain disorders are also not well understood—even by researchers—and do not yet have foolproof treatments. People who have a mental disorder or a disease or disorder that causes them to feel chronic pain can be the target of uninformed opinions. People who do not have these disorders sometimes struggle to understand how difficult it can be to deal with the symptoms. These disorders are often termed "invisible illnesses" because no one can see the symptoms; this leads many people to doubt that they exist or are serious problems. Additionally, people who have an undiagnosed disorder may understand that they are experiencing the world in a different way than their peers, but they have no one to turn to for answers.

Misinformation about all kinds of ailments is often spread through personal anecdotes, social media, and even news sources. This series aims to present accurate information about both physical and mental conditions so young adults will have a better understanding of them. Each volume discusses the symptoms of a particular disease or disorder, ways it is currently being treated, and the research that is being done to understand it further. Advice for people who may be suffering from a disorder is included, as well as information for their loved ones about how best to support them.

With fully cited quotes, a list of recommended books and websites for further research, and informational charts, this series provides young adults with a factual introduction to common illnesses. By learning more about these ailments, they will be better able to prevent the spread of contagious diseases, show compassion to people who are dealing with invisible illnesses, and take charge of their own health.

INTRODUCTION

MORE THAN JUST SADNESS

Depressive disorders—often simply referred to as depression—are common, but they are often misunderstood. Most people know that one component of depression is sadness, so many people say they are depressed when they mean that they simply feel less happy than usual. However, clinical depression is a disorder that goes far beyond normal sadness and can have a severe impact on a person's life. It is characterized by feelings of hopelessness and despair, as well as a loss of energy that makes completing normal tasks difficult or impossible. If it continues for long enough, depression can make people begin to think about suicide.

A depressive disorder interferes with daily life and causes pain for both the person with the disorder and those who care about him or her. One person diagnosed with depression described how it sapped their energy:

> *The things with depression that bother me the most are feeling like you're encased in cement, where you just can't drag your body out of bed, where the simplest of tasks is just daunting and you have to force yourself to re-focus and to pick yourself up and to take that shower, get to the grocery store, get the kids off to school, get to the office, get through your day.*[1]

Depression is a common but serious illness that affects more than 300 million people worldwide.

According to the Anxiety and Depression Association of America (ADAA), "In 2014, around 15.7 million adults age 18 or older in the [United States] had experienced at least one major depressive episode in the last year, which represented 6.7 percent of all American adults. At any point in time, 3 to 5 percent of adults suffer from major depression; the lifetime risk is about 17 percent. As many as 2 out of 100 young children and 8 out of 100 teens may have serious depression."[2] Fortunately, the vast majority of people can get better with treatment, which includes therapy and sometimes medication.

Millions of people suffer from depression, but it is still not well understood.

Depression has always existed, but its causes have never been fully understood. Many years ago, people believed that mental illnesses, including depression—or melancholia, as it was called then—were the result of an imbalance in bodily fluids. People also once thought mental illness was a sign of the devil. Throughout history, depression has also been viewed as a lack of willpower, laziness, or simply a disagreeable nature.

Today, depression is understood to have both situational and physical causes. Depression is different than grief or loneliness. When people are grieving, they mourn their loss but retain a certain sense of

Some situations, such as financial problems, can cause depression or make it worse.

self-esteem. Lonely people may be sad, but they do not have the sense of dread that is often associated with depression.

Depression is a mental illness that affects millions of people, sometimes in very different ways. Some people are able to continue going to school, to their jobs, and to the many other activities that they enjoy. However, for many, depression is a debilitating disease that stops them in their tracks. They find it difficult to get out of bed or to take care of themselves, let alone their family. The good news is that even for the most severe cases of depression, proper diagnosis and treatment can ensure a long, healthy, and productive life.

CHAPTER ONE

DEFINING DEPRESSION

Sadness is an uncomfortable feeling, but it is one that is part of life. Failing a test, losing a friend, suffering a disappointment, or hearing bad news are all things that can make someone feel sad. However, for people without a mental disorder, this sadness is temporary. It does not overwhelm the person's life and can easily be dealt with if the person does something to cheer themselves up, such as watching a favorite movie or talking to a friend. In contrast, for someone with depression, the feelings of sadness and hopelessness are much more intense than normal. Sometimes they react to events in a way that is disproportionate to the event; for instance, a simple thing such as losing a favorite item, which can be frustrating or sad for a person without a disorder, may cause someone with depression to feel extreme despair. Things that would normally cheer them up often lose their appeal, which makes it difficult for them to get rid of their negative feelings.

Frequently, people with depression report that there is no obvious cause for their feelings. This can make dealing with depression even more upsetting because the person is unsure why they are depressed, which means they have no idea what to do to fix the problem. They may feel guilty for being upset when everything in their life seems to be going fine, and they may be hesitant to share their feelings with others out of fear that they will be accused of being overdramatic.

Some people describe depression as a black hole or a curtain coming down over their life. People suffering from depression often see no hope. They may have a constant feeling of impending doom. In fact, some people with depression do not feel sad as much as numb, lifeless, or empty. They may be unable to experience any emotions at all.

Some people with depression feel numb and express no emotion, while others cry more than normal.

A Serious Disorder

Depression is on the rise around the world. In 1990, the Global Burden of Disease (GBD) study found major depression to be the fourth leading cause of disability worldwide. When the study was repeated in 2010, it was found to be the second leading cause of disability. As of 2017, according to the World Health Organization, it is the number one leading cause.

One reason for the level of disability is the sheer duration of depressive episodes. A major study of patients who required hospitalization for depression found that the median time to recover was five months. In other words, half of the people hospitalized for depression recovered in five months or less; the other half needed longer than five months. Another problem is that many people have recurring incidences of depression or continue to experience some residual symptoms of depression even after they are feeling better.

Depression is classified as a mood disorder, a term used for any disorder in which a disturbance in the person's mood is the main feature or problem. One of the most common and most serious types of depression is clinical depression, which is also called major depressive disorder. Other types of depression include dysthymia, seasonal affective disorder, postpartum depression, and bipolar disorder. These types of depression vary greatly in onset and severity.

Clinical Depression

Major depressive disorder, also known as clinical depression, is the most severe type of depression. People young and old suffer from clinical depression; the median age of onset is 32 years. People who have gone through an episode of depression are at risk for having another episode at one point or another. Some people experience recurring episodes of clinical depression throughout their lives.

Clinical depression prevents a person from functioning normally. It is characterized by a combination of symptoms that interfere with a person's ability to work, study, sleep, and eat. The signs and symptoms vary from one person to another. Many depressed people complain that they are constantly anxious or irritable. Concentration and memory problems are

Depression's Link with Anxiety

Depressive disorders and anxiety disorders often go hand in hand. According to the Anxiety and Depression Association of America (ADAA):

> *Depression and anxiety disorders are different, but people with depression often experience symptoms similar to those of an anxiety disorder, such as nervousness, irritability, and problems sleeping and concentrating. But each disorder has its own causes and its own emotional and behavioral symptoms.*
>
> *Many people who develop depression have a history of an anxiety disorder earlier in life. There is no evidence one disorder causes the other, but there is clear evidence that many people suffer from both disorders.*[1]

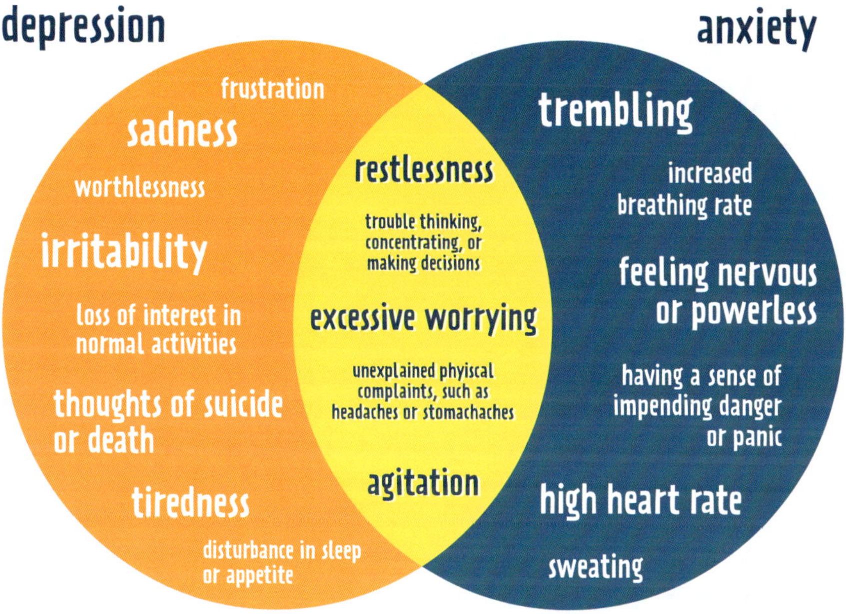

Depression and anxiety can share some symptoms but also have their own unique symptoms, as this information from Anxiety.org shows.

1. "Depression," Anxiety and Depression Association of America. www.adaa.org/understanding-anxiety/depression.

common, making tasks more difficult. People may not have energy to do much of anything, and activities that were once fun may no longer seem enjoyable. Some people have difficulty falling or staying asleep;

others sleep all the time. Some individuals lose their appetite, while others feel an overwhelming hunger. Often, people with clinical depression have little sense of self-worth and an overwhelming sense of dread or hopelessness.

Some people with depression sleep much more than usual.

Some people feel guilty for having depression or confused about why they are depressed when everything in their life seems to be going fine. Jared Padalecki, one of the stars of the TV show *Supernatural*, has been open about his struggle with the disorder. He described how he was diagnosed with depression after a breakdown during the filming of the third season of *Supernatural*:

> *It kind of hit me like a sack of bricks … I mean, I was 25 years old. I had my own TV show. I had dogs that I loved and tons of friends and I was getting adoration from fans and I was happy with my work, but I couldn't figure out what it was; it*

doesn't always make sense is my point. It's not just people who can't find a job, or can't fit in in society that struggle with depression sometimes … I say constantly that there's no shame in dealing with these things … There's no shame in having to fight every day … and presumably, if you're still alive to hear these words or read this interview, then you are winning your war. You're here.[3]

Padalecki has created T-shirts that say "Always Keep Fighting," and the proceeds from their sale go to support To Write Love On Her Arms, a nonprofit organization that aims to help people struggling with depression, self-harm, and thoughts of suicide.

Sometimes clinical depression comes with symptoms of psychosis; this is known as major depressive disorder with psychotic features, or psychotic depression. In this rarer form of depression, sufferers develop delusions or hallucinations. They might think they are already dead or that they are responsible for war, hunger, or natural disaster. They might hear voices saying they are worthless or urging suicide or other destructive behavior. According to the National Alliance on Mental Illness (NAMI), about one in five people with major depressive disorder develop symptoms of psychosis, and people with a family history of mental illness are more at risk. Brain scans of patients with this form of depression suggest that the disease may be due to a brain abnormality. Most people suffering from psychotic depression do not recover without treatment. The most successful treatment of this kind of depression involves antidepressant and antipsychotic medications.

Dysthymic Disorder

Dysthymia, also called dysthymic disorder or persistent depressive disorder, is a less severe form of depression. The word "dysthymia" comes from a Greek term meaning "ill humor or bad mood." Dysthymia is a chronic form of depression that affects 1.5 percent of the adult U.S. population, according to the National Institute of Mental Health (NIMH).

The symptoms of dysthymia are similar to but less severe than those associated with major depressive disorder. Life seems gray and uninteresting. People with dysthymia generally feel mildly depressed on most days over a period of at least two months. Studies show that dysthymia generally has a gradual onset, often in people in their late teens or early 20s with a family history of depression. People who are socially isolated or who lack strong support groups are particularly vulnerable.

Although its symptoms are less debilitating, dysthymia is a serious form of depression. It rarely goes away without being treated with drugs, therapy, or a combination of both. Dysthymia can occur alone or with more severe depression. According to the Mayo Clinic, "major depression episodes may occur before or during persistent depressive disorder—this is sometimes called double depression."[4]

In *Depression and Bipolar Disorder*, psychiatrist Virginia Edwards described Martin, a hardworking executive who suffered from dysthymia. Martin was somewhat difficult to get along with at work, but he was a valued employee because he ran the office efficiently. Like many people with dysthymia, Martin rarely went out socially. He tended to find fault with his friends and the women to whom he was introduced. "Martin can't remember a time when he felt relaxed and happy," Edwards wrote. "He is always anticipating trouble and worried about the future. He thinks other people must feel the same way but manage to hide it better."[5] Although everyone feels blue sometimes, people such as Martin experience these feelings nearly constantly. It may not stop them from performing their daily tasks, but it seriously affects how much they enjoy life.

As with other forms of depression, the exact cause of dysthymia is unknown. Experts believe it may be due to one or more factors such as an imbalance in brain chemistry, genetics, or certain life events, such as the death of a loved one or prolonged stress from work, school, or financial troubles.

Seasonal Mood Changes

Several other depression-related mood disorders are triggered by specific aspects of a person's environment. Seasonal affective disorder (SAD), for instance, is characterized by depressive episodes that occur only during the winter months, when there is less sunlight. Differences in mood are common ailments: People often talk of the "winter blues" or "cabin fever" they get when cooped up all winter. SAD is typically diagnosed when these mood changes are severe and when they occur over two or more seasons. Although SAD is generally considered a "winter" disease, a rarer form of the disorder affects people during the summer months.

Seasonal affective disorder makes people feel depressed during winter, when the days are shorter and there is less sunlight than normal.

SAD has been linked to a biochemical imbalance in the brain prompted by less daylight. Sufferers experience many of the same symptoms as those with major depression, but the SAD patient almost always has an increase in sleep, complaining of chronic fatigue throughout the winter months. In addition, an increase in appetite rather than a decrease is more common; SAD patients may gain weight each winter. Many SAD sufferers report food cravings, particularly for sweets and carbohydrates. With SAD, these symptoms generally go away during the spring and summer months. Approximately 500,000 American adults seek treatment for SAD each year.

Depression after Giving Birth

Another common situational type of depression is postpartum or postnatal depression. This term is used to describe a major depressive episode experienced by a mother after having a baby. Postpartum depression generally occurs in the first few weeks after giving birth, but for some women, the onset may come several months after delivery. In addition to changes in hormone levels, experts cite sleep deprivation, increased stress that comes from having to care for a baby, and a loss of the sense of self and control over one's self as contributing factors to postpartum depression.

In *Glamour* magazine, model Chrissy Teigen described her depression following the birth of her baby: "After I had Luna, our home was under construction, so we lived in a rental home, then a hotel, and I blamed whatever stress or detachment or sadness I was feeling at that time on the fact that there were so many odd circumstances."[6] Teigen assumed she would bounce back when she and her family moved back into their house, but her feelings intensified and began to affect her work: "Getting out of bed to get to set on time was painful. My lower back throbbed;

my shoulders—even my wrists—hurt. I didn't have an appetite."[7] She described how she was quick to lose her temper and yell at people who asked her questions; then she would feel upset about it afterward. When she was not at work, she stayed in the house, trying to work up the energy to move off the couch. She had severe pain and nausea, which went unexplained until a doctor finally realized she had all the symptoms of postpartum depression as well as anxiety.

With therapy and antidepressants, Teigen's symptoms did not completely disappear, but they improved dramatically. She mentioned that it took so long for her to be diagnosed because she did not know much about postpartum depression: "Before this, I had never, ever—in my whole entire life—had one person say to me: 'I have postpartum depression.' Growing up in the nineties, I associated postpartum depression with … people who didn't like their babies or felt like they had to harm their children. I didn't have anything remotely close to those feelings. I looked at Luna every day, amazed by her. So I didn't think I had it."[8] This illustrates that people can experience depression in a variety of different ways.

Some new mothers develop depression, which may make it difficult for them to care for and bond with their child.

Postpartum depression is estimated to affect 10 to 15 percent of new mothers. Studies show that women who experience postpartum depression often have had prior depressive episodes and are more likely to experience major depression later in life. Additionally, women who experience postpartum depression after one birth are more likely to have a recurring episode after subsequent births. The symptoms are the same as with any major depressive episode, but postpartum depression can sometimes interfere with the mother's ability to care for and bond with her newborn. This can lead to intense feelings of guilt and shame, as these women often assume they are bad mothers for not being able to feel love and joy for their child. However, these feelings are not their fault, and treatment can help them overcome negative emotions and begin experiencing positive ones.

Ups and Downs

Major depression, dysthymia, and SAD are all characterized by intense lows. These forms of depression are sometimes called unipolar depression to differentiate them from bipolar disorder, a mood disorder in which the lows alternate with highs. Sometimes people can swing rapidly between moods, but generally, the change from one mood to another is fairly gradual. One sufferer described the symptoms:

> *If you have bipolar [disorder] as I do … you wear many faces. You are either the life of the party and feel that life is wonderful and so much fun, only to wake up the next day so depressed you think you won't make it until the next day. Then within a few hours or 6 months, you are screaming at the top of your voice, feeling extremely out of control, extremely irritable and you want to smash everybody and everything around you.*[9]

Roughly 5.7 million American adults—2.6 percent—have been diagnosed with bipolar disorder. Bipolar disorder differs from other forms of depression in both causes and treatments. Unlike unipolar depression, bipolar disorder almost always requires medical treatment for life.

Risk Factors for Clinical Depression

Although clinical depression can affect anyone, certain people are more at risk than others. Some of the risk factors include:

- *Certain personality traits, such as low self-esteem and being too dependent, self-critical or pessimistic*
- *Traumatic or stressful events, such as physical or sexual abuse, the death or loss of a loved one, a difficult relationship, or financial problems*
- *Childhood trauma or depression that started when you were a teen or child*
- *Blood relatives with a history of depression, bipolar disorder, alcoholism or suicide*
- *Being lesbian, gay, bisexual or transgender in an unsupportive situation*
- *History of other mental health disorders, such as anxiety disorder, eating disorders or post-traumatic stress disorder*
- *Abuse of alcohol or illegal drugs*
- *Serious or chronic illness, including cancer, stroke, chronic pain or heart disease*
- *Certain medications, such as some high blood pressure medications or sleeping pills (talk to your doctor before stopping any medication)*[10]

Many of these are risk factors for other types of depression as well. For instance, many researchers believe that genetics plays a strong role in all types of depression. So far, no research has shown a specific gene or genes to be responsible for the disorder; most scientists today believe that the risk for depression results from the influence of multiple genes acting together with environmental or other factors. However, having a family history of depression does not automatically mean someone will develop the disorder.

Gender and Depression

Women and men can both become depressed, but women are almost twice as likely to be diagnosed with depression. Some experts believe this is because

The Dementors

In J.K. Rowling's Harry Potter series, dementors are creatures that feed on happiness. If they get too close to a person, he or she will feel extreme coldness, sadness, and despair. In the words of Hagrid, one of the characters, after his stay in Azkaban, the dementor-guarded wizard prison, "Thought I was goin' mad. Kep' goin' over horrible stuff in me mind … Yeh can' really remember who yeh are after a while. An' yeh can' see the point o' livin' at all. I used ter hope I'd jus' die in me sleep … When they let me out, it was like bein' born again, ev'rythin' came floodin' back, it was the bes' feeling in the world."[1]

Rowling has stated that the dementors are based on her own experience with depression. While she started writing the Harry Potter series, she was a young, single mother on the brink of poverty. The stress of this greatly contributed to her depression. She said it "was characterized by a numbness, a coldness and an inability to believe you will feel happy again. All the color drained out of life."[2]

Some people feel that depression is caused by a lack of willpower—that someone should be able to just "snap out of it." This can make people who are depressed feel ashamed or guilty for the way they feel, even though it is not their fault and they desperately want to feel better. However, Rowling has said, "I have never been remotely ashamed of having been depressed. Never. What's there to be ashamed of? I went through a really tough time and I am quite proud that I got out of that."[3]

1. J.K. Rowling, *Harry Potter and the Prisoner of Azkaban*. New York, NY: Scholastic, 1999, pp. 220-221.

2. Quoted in Margaret Lenker, "5 Times J.K. Rowling Got Real About Depression," The Mighty, August 1, 2015. themighty.com/2015/08/5-times-j-k-rowling-got-real-about-depression/.

women are more likely to seek help than men; others believe women may be at higher risk due partly to hormonal changes brought on by puberty, menstruation, menopause, and pregnancy. Research has shown that hormones directly affect the parts of the brain that control mood. The risk of depression increases with menopause and menstruation, for instance. Scientists believe that the rise and fall of estrogen and other hormones may affect the brain chemistry that is associated with depressive illness. For instance, many women experience premenstrual syndrome (PMS), a condition that happens a few days before their period starts. It is common for women with PMS to feel sad, angry, or anxious over things that would not normally upset them. These symptoms are generally mild, last only a few days, and go away after their period starts. However, between 3 and 8 percent of menstruating women experience a condition called premenstrual dysphoric disorder (PMDD).

The dementors in the Harry Potter series came from J.K. Rowling's past experience with depression.

3. Quoted in Lenker, "5 Times J.K. Rowling Got Real About Depression."

PMDD is a form of PMS that lasts longer and has more severe symptoms, some of which can seriously disrupt a woman's daily life. Symptoms include intense, uncontrollable anger; depression characterized by feelings of hopelessness and sometimes suicidal thoughts; mood swings; anxiety; difficulty concentrating; changes in appetite; and changes in sleep patterns (suddenly sleeping too much or too little). These symptoms begin when a woman starts ovulating—when a woman's body releases an egg—and last up to two weeks, when she begins her period. In order for PMDD to be diagnosed, the woman must have at least seven days each month when she does not experience symptoms. Researchers are not sure exactly what causes PMDD, but they believe lower than normal levels of serotonin may be to blame. PMDD can cause severe depression, and it can also make an existing depressive disorder worse.

Societal and environmental factors may also play a role. The stress of balancing work and home responsibilities; caring for young children, aging parents, or both; abuse; poverty; and dealing with difficult relationships may all increase the risk of depression.

The risk for depression is lower for men than for women, but men are by no means immune to the disorder. More than 6 million American men are treated for depression each year. Some experts suggest that the number of men with depression may actually be much higher because many men do not seek help. Although depression and other mental illnesses do not have the stigma they once did, many men still believe that asking for help for emotional problems is a sign of weakness.

Men also react to depressive feelings differently than women. Men are more likely to become hostile or violent. Others may turn to drugs or alcohol to deal with their feelings of despair or

Men may be less likely to seek help for depression because society tells them they should not show signs of anything that might be considered emotional weakness. In reality, however, having depression does not make a person weak.

hopelessness. They may throw themselves into their work to avoid having to focus on their feelings, or they may engage in risky recreational pursuits, extreme sports, or reckless behavior. Suicide is an especially serious risk for men with depression. Although more women attempt suicide, men are four times more likely than women to succeed.

Depression in Young People

Until recently, many doctors and other professionals did not believe children could be depressed. However, recent research shows that although the onset of depression is typically between the ages of 20 and 40, young adults can also experience depression. According to NIMH, "In 2015, an estimated 3 million adolescents aged 12 to 17 in the United States had at least one major depressive episode in the past year. This number represented 12.5 [percent] of the U.S. population aged 12 to 17."[11]

Unfortunately, depression in young people often goes undiagnosed. Parents often assume that the signs of depression are a result of a poor attitude, laziness, or simply a phase of growing up. Extreme moods are common for teens as a result of changing hormones, but when depression lingers for weeks or months, it can affect school performance, relationships with friends and family, sleep, and appetite. Left untreated, childhood depression often continues into adulthood. Many people who have minor depression as children will experience more severe illnesses in adulthood.

As children, boys and girls are equally likely to develop depressive disorders. By age 15, however, girls are nearly three times as likely as boys to have had a major depressive episode. Some experts believe the higher rate among adolescent girls may be due to both biology and environmental factors. Changes in the levels of female hormones during puberty may be to blame. In addition, according to Dr. Barbara Greenberg,

> *As girls approach the early teen years they begin to understand from various sources including media and peers how much their appearance is judged and valued by others. When they were younger there was clearly less emphasis on their attractiveness, appearance, and sexuality. Now, in their teen years, there is pressure for them not only to do well socially and academically but also to meet societal standards of what is considered both sexy and attractive. They experience all of these pressures within the context of monthly hormonal upheavals which may occur at regular or irregular intervals.*[12]

Adolescence brings on many physical and emotional changes. Breaking away from one's parents, making decisions on one's own, grappling with issues related to dating, dealing with peer pressure, deciding where to go to college or what to do with one's future—these are just a few of the stresses teens face. Additionally, teens who are struggling with issues such as racism, homophobia, poverty, and bullying have extra stressors in their lives. Many experts believe these stressors contribute to the risk of clinical depression for both

Percentage of Persons Ages 12 and Over with Depression, by Poverty Status and Race and Hispanic Origin: United States, 2009–2012

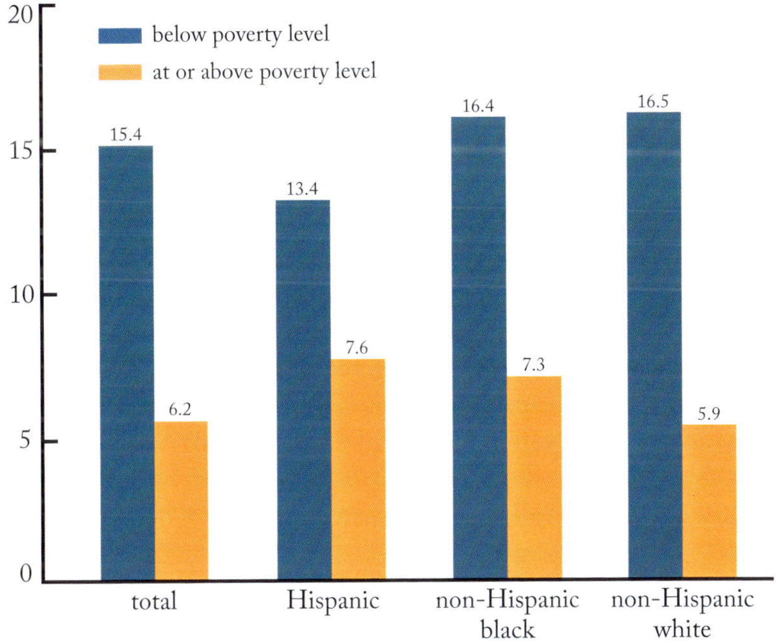

Poverty and race may play a role in a young person's level of depression, as this information from the Centers for Disease Control and Prevention (CDC) suggests.

boys and girls. Depression among teens frequently coincides with anxiety, eating disorders, or substance abuse. It also increases the risk of teen suicide.

Effects on Health

Depression can have a major impact on sufferers' health. People with depression are at greater risk of developing other physical illnesses. Experts caution that those suffering from depression may be less likely to go to the doctor when they are sick or to take the doctor's advice. Research also suggests that depression and the resulting stress weaken the immune system and reduce its ability to fight infection.

Recent studies have also shown that people with depression who are recovering from serious illnesses have more difficulty making health care choices, following a doctor's instructions, and coping with the challenges that such illnesses present. Studies also have linked depression to heart disease.

Chronic illness may lead to depression or increase its severity, in part because of the weakness and stress that accompany a serious medical condition. Just getting through the day can be difficult for people who are in constant pain or have a disability that prevents them from doing what they want to do.

The more severe the symptoms of depression, the greater the impact on a person's day-to-day life. People suffering from a mild form of the illness might be able to continue their usual activities, although they might not find them quite as enjoyable. As depression takes hold, however, it might take more and more effort to get up in the morning, leave the house, and concentrate at school or work. In severe cases of depression, any activity can become difficult.

Another health risk associated with depression is alcohol and drug abuse and addiction. Research has been inconclusive about whether one of those disorders causes the other or whether they share genetic or environmental risk factors. Experts have long believed that people suffering from depression may "self-medicate" with alcohol or drugs to alleviate the symptoms. A 2004 study by the U.S. Department of Health and Human Services reported that teens with depression were almost twice as likely to use alcohol, illegal drugs, and cigarettes as those who did not have depression. Other research—including a 25-year study by scientists in New Zealand—concludes that alcohol abuse or dependence increases the risk of developing clinical depression.

Similarly, depression is sometimes associated with the use of illegal recreational drugs, such as marijuana, ecstasy, and heroin. As with alcohol, a person who is suffering from depressive symptoms may take drugs

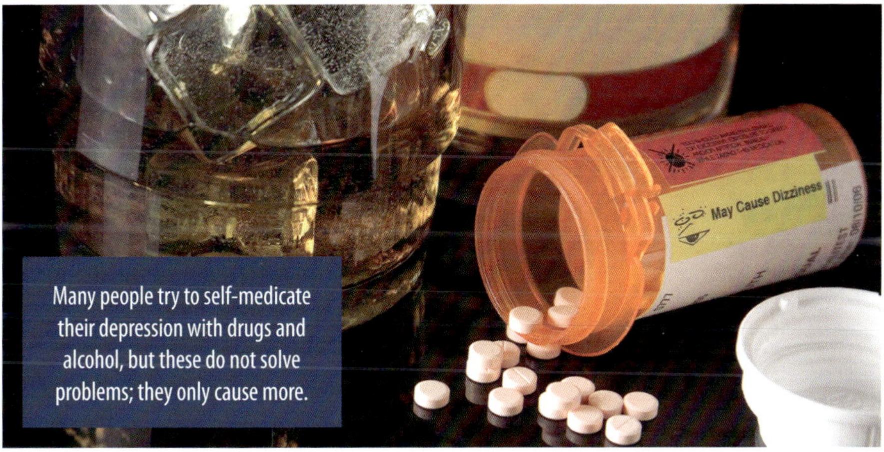

Many people try to self-medicate their depression with drugs and alcohol, but these do not solve problems; they only cause more.

in the hope of gaining some relief, or depressive symptoms may develop as a direct result of taking drugs. In some cases, depression is a symptom of withdrawal when a person stops taking a drug.

Drugs and alcohol may seem like a way to cope with depressive symptoms, but they lead to deeper problems. Someone may feel better temporarily while they are drunk or high, but over time, alcohol and drugs can make depression symptoms worse. This can lead to addiction—the person wants to be under the influence all the time to keep the symptoms from coming back. Becoming dependent on drugs and alcohol can further damage someone's sense of self-worth and add to physical health problems, as well as problems with work, school, and relationships.

Suicide is another risk associated with depression. Most people who suffer from depression do not attempt suicide, but this is a very real danger, particularly for those who do not seek treatment. Mental Health America reports that an estimated 30 to 70 percent of suicide victims have suffered from some form of depression, and according to the Centers for Disease Control and Prevention (CDC), suicide is the third leading cause of death for people between the ages of 15 and 24.

Depression Affects Everyone

Depression affects not only the person who is suffering from the disorder, but also their family and friends. At home, people with depression sometimes lack interest in or concern for their family and friends. They may often find it hard to demonstrate affection for loved ones. They may avoid friends and social gatherings.

Living with someone with depression can be very difficult. Depression often strains relationships with family members. Friendships may crumble. As family members and friends become more distant, the person with depression may feel abandoned and even more worthless, worsening the depression.

Depression can also have an effect on society at large. At work, people with depression tend to be slower and less productive than healthier individuals. They also tend to be indecisive and uncertain. The inability to concentrate may result in more mistakes. Depression can also cause people to miss work. People suffering from major depression sometimes find it hard to get out of bed in the morning and may be likely to take more sick leave. Depression can also cause headaches, stomachaches, or chronic pain, which may result in missed work. All of this lost time and missed work can create additional stress for someone already suffering from depression. They may encounter financial troubles or be worried about losing their job.

Experts have studied depression's impact on workers. Research from Gallup, a public opinion poll website, found that full-time workers in the United States with major depression—about 10.8 percent of the full-time workforce—lost an average of 8.7 workdays per year, while those without depression generally lose only 4.6. The study also found that rates of depression and missed workdays were higher for part-time workers: "16.6 percent of part-time workers have ever been depressed, and they miss an average of 13.7 work days per year due to poor health, compared to 8.7 absences among part-time employees with no history of depression."[13] Altogether, the missed work and the decreased productivity cost U.S. businesses about $23 billion a year.

The medical costs of depression also go beyond medication and therapy. Many depressed people have unexplained pain or illnesses. They go to the doctor seeking relief from the symptoms, but the problem often remains untreated. As the issue is unresolved, the visits to the doctor—and expenses—continue to add up. In addition, people with depression may ignore medical problems because they find it difficult to work up the energy to deal with them. This can lead to more problems and expenses later on, particularly if the depression is left untreated for a prolonged period of time.

Fortunately, depression can be improved with treatment. Mental health advocates urge businesses to have employee assistance programs where employees can get help for their problems and health insurance that will reduce financial obstacles. Still, many people suffering from depression do not get help. In some cases, people are ashamed to admit they have a problem. Others might fail to recognize the symptoms of depression, especially if they are mild. People may try to explain away their symptoms or downplay their feelings, which means the symptoms often continue to get worse.

The sense of hopelessness that is symptomatic of depression can be an obstacle for the very people most in need of treatment. Some people with depression may lack the energy needed to make a phone call or keep an appointment with a doctor or therapist. The first step is to recognize the warning signs and understand the many factors that can contribute to depression.

CHAPTER TWO

THE TRUTH ABOUT DEPRESSION

Just as with other mental illnesses, many myths about depression persist in society. It is difficult for someone who has never experienced depression to understand how hard it can be to deal with. Physical ailments have a visible cause, but mental illnesses are generally invisible, so some people either do not believe they exist or downplay their seriousness. They may believe that people who have depression are weak, lazy, selfish, or attention-seeking; that depression is not a real mental illness; or that someone who has no obvious reason to be depressed should be able to simply get over it. However, all of these beliefs are false.

Depression is a serious mental illness that can have severe effects on the life of a sufferer and their loved ones. It is not a sign of weakness; on the contrary, facing each day in spite of feelings of sadness, despair, and low self-worth takes incredible strength. Society's negative attitudes toward depression can make people feel worse about what they are experiencing or avoid seeking treatment, so it is important for people to understand the truth about this disorder.

Brain Chemistry and Depression

Although depression can be caused by specific situations, such as financial problems or being the victim of bullying, it can also appear to happen for no reason. Researchers believe the problem is an unexplained imbalance of chemicals in the brain. Like a complex

Hyperbole and a Half

Cartoonist Allie Brosh has a blog and a book called *Hyperbole and a Half* in which she talks about her struggle with depression, often in a humorous way. In one blog post, she described what her depression felt like and talked about how frustrating it was when people who were not depressed were unable to understand that she could not simply cheer herself up:

> *At first, I'd try to explain that it's not really negativity or sadness anymore, it's more just this detached, meaningless fog where you can't feel anything about anything—even the things you love, even fun things—and you're horribly bored and lonely, but since you've lost your ability to connect with any of the things that would normally make you feel less bored and lonely, you're stuck in the boring, lonely, meaningless void without anything to distract you from how boring, lonely, and meaningless it is ... And that's the most frustrating thing about depression. It isn't always something you can fight back against with hope. It isn't even something—it's nothing. And you can't combat nothing. You can't fill it up. You can't cover it ... It would be like having a bunch of dead fish, but no one around you will acknowledge that the fish are dead. Instead, they offer to help you look for the fish or try to help you figure out why they disappeared ... The problem might not even have a solution. But you aren't necessarily looking for solutions. You're maybe just looking for someone to say "sorry about how dead your fish are" or "wow, those are super dead. I still like you, though."*[1]

1. Allie Brosh, "Depression Part Two," *Hyperbole and a Half*, May 9, 2013. hyperboleandahalf.blogspot.com/2013/05/depression-part-two.html.

computer, the human brain serves as the "command center" of the human body. The brain controls basic automatic, unconscious functions, such as the heart's pumping of blood through the body. A small structure at the base of the brain called the hypothalamus automatically regulates body temperature, sleep, and appetite. The brain also controls emotions and mood.

Neurons and neurotransmitters play an important role in the processes of the body. Neurons are nerve cells in the brain that are organized to control specialized activities. In the brain, 100 billion neurons transmit messages from one to another in the form of chemicals, called neurotransmitters, which carry the messages through the synapses—the narrow gaps that separate the neurons. These chemical messengers travel across the neurons at less than 1/5,000 of a second, allowing people to react instantaneously and unconsciously to pain or other stimuli.

Neurotransmitters "travel from neuron to neuron in an orderly fashion. They are specifically shaped so that after they pass from a neuron into the synapse, they can be received onto certain sites, called receptors, on a neighboring neuron."[14] Upon landing at the receptor site, the neurotransmitter may either be changed into an electrical impulse and continue on its way through the next neuron, or it may stop where it is. In either case, the neurotransmitter leaves the receptor site and floats back into the synapse. There, it can either be broken down by a chemical, or it can be reabsorbed by the neuron that initially released it, a process called reuptake.

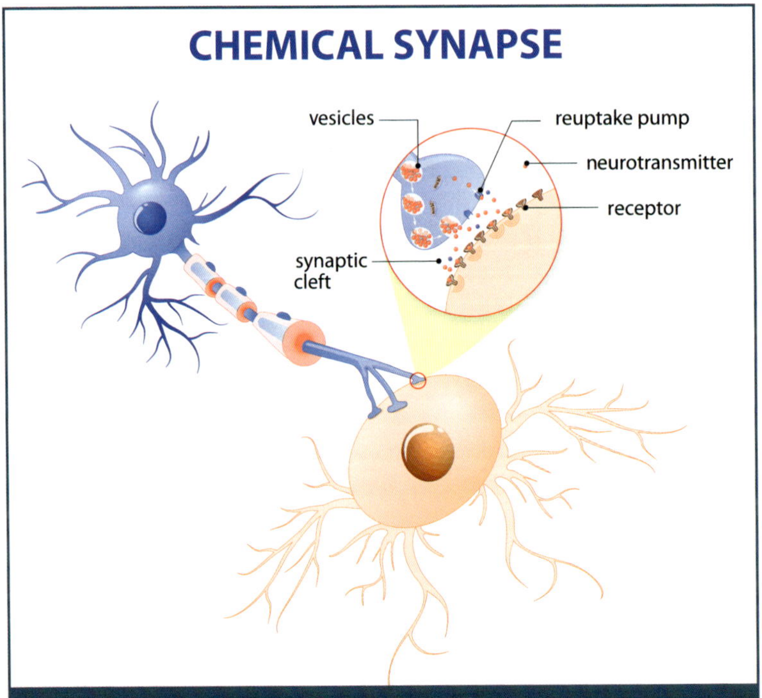

This diagram shows how neurotransmitters travel.

Research has shown that some forms of mental illness occur when too many or too few neurotransmitters are present or when a problem interferes with the way the neurotransmitters are released or broken down. Unfortunately, neurotransmitters are difficult to study because they exist only in very small quantities and disappear very quickly once they are used, but research has begun to yield some information about how neurotransmitters might influence emotions and behavior. Of the roughly 30 neurotransmitters that scientists have identified, 3 may play a particular role in depression: serotonin, norepinephrine, and dopamine. These three neurotransmitters help regulate emotions, reactions to stress, sleep, appetite, and sex.

Serotonin was among the first neurotransmitters to be identified and linked to depression. High levels of serotonin are associated with aggression and poor sleep quality. Low levels are associated with irritability, anxiety, lethargy, and suicidal thoughts and behaviors. Brain-imaging studies confirm that the transporter involved in regulating serotonin varies by season, leading scientists to speculate that imbalances of serotonin caused by too much or too little sunlight may be responsible for SAD. Many of the popular antidepressant medications on the market today act to increase the amount of serotonin in the brain.

Dopamine has also been linked to depression. Dopamine influences emotion, motor movements, learning, thinking, memory, and attention. Too little dopamine can contribute to depression.

The link between these neurotransmitters and depression is not always clear, however. Research has shown that many people who are depressed have low levels of norepinephrine, for instance, which regulates the "fight-or-flight" response to perceived danger in the environment. Although scientists have associated a low level of this neurotransmitter with depression, some people with clinical depression have unusually high levels. Experts caution that this also may be true for other neurotransmitters. Researchers disagree about the cause-and-effect relationship between neurotransmitters and depression. They are not sure whether a low level of one of these chemicals causes depression or whether it is depression that lowers the amount of the chemical.

Scientists also believe that other abnormalities in the brain may cause depression. Studies using brain-imaging technologies, such as magnetic resonance imaging (MRI), have shown that the brains of people who have depression look different than those of people without depression. For instance, the hippocampus—a specialized area of the brain involved in memory and emotion—is smaller in people with chronic depression.

The Role of Hormones

Research has shown that many people who are depressed have abnormal levels of some hormones. Changes in hormones are thought to play a major role in postpartum depression, for instance. It is believed that abnormal levels of some hormones—or rapid fluctuations in these levels—may result in depressive symptoms such as problems with appetite and sleeping.

About half of those individuals who are clinically depressed have an excess of the hormone cortisol in their blood. Cortisol is secreted by the adrenal glands. Located on the kidneys, the adrenal glands influence reactions to stressful events. Scientists believe that cortisol may be related to depression because as symptoms of depression disappear, the levels of this hormone often return to normal. Scientists also believe that abnormal levels of hormones, such as testosterone in men and progesterone and estrogen in women, may be the culprits in the onset of some types of depression.

The relationship between hormones and depression has led scientists to believe the endocrine system may play an important role in the disease. The endocrine system is the system of small glands that create hormones and release them into the bloodstream. The endocrine system is connected with the brain at the hypothalamus. A healthy endocrine system keeps hormone levels at a relatively constant state through feedback processes, much like a thermostat in a home. When the endocrine system is not functioning properly, the brain may fail to receive the message that sufficient amounts of hormones are already in the bloodstream. The adrenal glands—which are part of the endocrine system—may continue to secrete hormones without regard to the amount that is already in the blood. Scientists believe this malfunction results in many of the symptoms characteristic of depression.

Depression also may be a symptom of a disorder or disease in the organs that produce hormones. Conditions such as thyroid disorders, Cushing's syndrome, and Addison's disease can increase a person's risk of depression.

Breaking the Silence

Despite the fact that so many people suffer from depression, those who suffer from it are often hesitant to talk about it. They may be embarrassed, feel they should be able to get over it themselves, have a negative view of people who go to therapy, or worry about pushing their loved ones away. The myths surrounding depression, such as the idea that it is not a real mental illness or that it is easy to overcome with willpower, contribute to this culture of silence.

Many celebrities have begun to speak out in recent years about their battle with depression and have encouraged others to do the same. Kristen Bell, the voice of Anna in the film *Frozen*, has been especially outspoken about ending this stigma, or negative perception. She revealed on the *Today* show why she decided to make her struggle public: "I was talking with my husband, and it occurred to me that I do appear to be very bubbly and positive … I've never really shared what got me there and why I'm that way or the things that I've worked through. And I felt it was sort of a social responsibility I had—to not just appear to be so positive and optimistic."[15] This shows people who have dealt with depression sometimes hide it very well, and just because someone appears to be happy does not mean they are not suffering.

Kristen Bell has said that although she often appears to be happy, she has struggled with depression most of her life.

Depression is a personal thing, and people are not required to tell everyone about it. However, telling a few close friends or family members is important because a strong support network makes overcoming depression much easier, and telling people is the first step toward getting the proper treatment. Someone who is depressed or suicidal should identify the people they trust most, such as their parents or best friends—people who will be compassionate and helpful, rather than judgmental.

Picking the right time and place is also important; ideally, it should be when everyone is calm and in a private place where the person with depression feels safe. This can sometimes be difficult, as the person's negative feelings can become overwhelming. If the conversation gets too intense, it can be paused and resumed at a later time.

A person who was chosen to be told about their loved one's depression should validate the other person's feelings by saying things such as, "I still love you," "I'm here for you," and "I'm glad you told me." They can also ask questions such as, "What can I do to help?," "Did something happen to make you start feeling like this?," and "Have you tried anything to make you feel better?" They should listen carefully to the answers rather than giving advice the person may not want or need.

The Threat of Suicide

One of the most tragic consequences of depression is the high risk of suicide that goes along with the disorder. Some mental health professionals believe untreated depression to be the largest cause of suicide. Suicide is the eighth leading cause of death in the United States, and almost all people who take their own lives have a diagnosable mental disorder. Suicide rates are higher among people with depression who also drink alcohol or take drugs.

Some antidepressants can actually have the effect of making people feel suicidal, especially in people under the age of 18. Some experts speculate that this may be because people with severe depression lack the energy to commit suicide. As people respond to antidepressants or other types of treatment, there may be a period in which they still feel a sense of hopelessness but now have more energy. Others believe it is a consequence of the way the medications alter brain chemistry. Close monitoring of severely depressed patients by family, friends, and medical professionals, particularly during the early phases of treatment, can help reduce the risk of suicide.

According to Mental Health America, most people who commit suicide have talked about suicide or previously tried to kill themselves. Some people believe that a person who talks about suicide is being overdramatic and seeking attention, which often leads them to dismiss the person's distress. However, "people who hurt themselves in what they view as a suicide attempt do so because of great pain, desperation, or other distressing emotions. If they are crying out for help, there is usually a good reason for them to do so—and a good reason for others to listen."[16] Someone who talks about wanting to commit suicide should always be taken seriously.

Some people show indirect signs of being suicidal. These include:

- making statements about how people would benefit if they were no longer around
- increased drug and alcohol use
- taking risks
- showing aggression or violence
- not taking care of themselves
- giving away their possessions
- reconnecting with old friends "one last time."

If a loved one is exhibiting these signs, their friends and family should start a conversation about whether there is anything the person needs help dealing with.

Some people believe that those who commit suicide are weak or cowardly because they are no longer able to face their problems and selfish because their death causes pain for their loved ones. However, someone who is suicidal is simply trying to find a way out of a situation that seems hopeless and is tired of feeling overwhelmed every day. They often believe they are a burden on their friends and family, so they do not see suicide as a selfish act. However, it is important for people who are thinking of suicide to remember that it is a permanent solution to a temporary problem and that their death would be devastating to their loved ones. One blogger, Jenny Lawson, writes often about her struggle with mental illness, including severe depression. She frequently reminds her readers that depression lies—in other words, the negative things they think when they are depressed are untrue:

> *I've learned that I'm not alone even when I feel completely isolated and like a failure. I've learned that depression lies. I've learned that when I'm not affected by my … brain chemistry I can see that my brain is not to be trusted so I write notes to myself when I'm out of the hole to remind myself that I'll be okay again soon … I laugh loudly and often when I'm out of the hole because I know the importance of appreciating the good and the joy when it comes.*[17]

Blogger Jenny Lawson often encourages her followers to remain hopeful with the phrase, "Depression lies."

Mental Illness Is Not Desirable

Although suicide is not necessarily a cowardly act, it is not brave or noble either. Experts have noted a disturbing trend in the past decade of young people using social media websites such as Tumblr to post things that romanticize depression and suicide, or make them seem better than they actually are. According to *The Atlantic*, "Today the depression many teenagers … say they have is one that's linked to a notion of 'beautiful' suffering."[18] These teens share pictures and text posts that make having depression seem glamorous; the idea behind them is often that depression helps people understand life better than others or that there is some greater purpose to it that makes their sadness seem worth it. Some posts romanticize suicide, making it seem like an easy and poetic escape from suffering.

There are several problems with romanticizing depression and suicide. In the first place, many people who do so do not suffer from a depressive disorder. Because the term "depression" is used so casually, people often do not truly understand what it means. According to Dr. Stan Kutcher, an adolescent psychiatry expert, "You see kids self-identifying as having that depression, but they don't have a depression. They're upset, or they're demoralized, or they're distressed by something."[19] This is very different than having clinical depression; these feelings are a part of life that everyone experiences, but romanticizing them on social media makes them seem like huge obstacles that can never be overcome. Sharing these posts repeatedly reinforces the idea that, rather than being a treatable mental illness, clinical depression is a typical part of the teen experience, so nothing will help and there is no point in trying to feel better.

According to *The Atlantic*, girls are more affected by this issue than boys:

[Dr. Mark Reinecke, chief psychologist at Northwestern Memorial Hospital,] proposes an explanation for this: girls and boys in modern society are socialized differently. Boys are socialized to take action. While not always helpful in managing their problems, it helps get their mind off them for a time. Girls are pushed to dwell on their experience.

"What you can get sometimes is a reverberating 'echo chamber' of girls who are sharing these experiences and these thoughts and it potentiates [increases the effect of] the negative feelings, the depression … Teenagers will say, 'My friends understand me. They get it,'" Reinecke says. "All right, good, but when you're with them, does it lead you to feel better? Do they give you a different perspective on the world, or different things that you could try to improve things? The answer is: 'Well, no, but they do understand me.'"[20]

This kind of attitude encourages people not to even try to feel better. If they do start to feel better—especially if they do have clinical depression and begin getting help for it—their change in outlook may cause problems with friends who are still romanticizing depression. It may also lead to accusations of previously faking their depression. It can be difficult

Some people share posts online that romanticize depression and suicide, trying to make suffering seem beautiful. However, these posts mask the seriousness of these issues.

for people to understand that sometimes personality changes are a result of lifestyle changes, and that getting treatment generally leads to a natural improvement in mood. Someone who becomes happier after receiving therapy or medication was not faking their depression previously; they are simply responding positively to their treatment.

What Not to Say

People who do not suffer from depression often become frustrated with people who do because they are unable to understand how difficult it is for the sufferer to deal with what is happening to them. Sometimes people say things to try to make a loved one feel better, but often, the words they believe are comforting actually make the person with depression feel worse. Some things that are generally not helpful for someone with depression to hear include:

- "What do you have to be depressed about?"
- "Just think positive thoughts."
- "Everyone gets sad; you need to learn how to deal with it."
- "Other people have worse problems."
- "You're still in bed? You're so lazy!"
- "Stop feeling sorry for yourself."
- "It's all in your head."
- "It seems like you're not even trying to feel better."
- "Have you tried just not being depressed?"
- "You used to be so cheerful. What happened to you?"
- "Things will get better eventually."
- "You'll definitely feel better if you [do yoga/meditate/exercise/etc.]."

Depression Is Treatable

To someone with depression, it may seem like nothing will ever make them feel better. However, there are several effective methods of treatment. Because researchers are still not completely sure what causes depression, there is not one specific cure for it. Instead, individuals can try a variety of treatment options to find the combination that works best for them. It takes hard work and determination, but the vast majority of people who have received treatment say it is worth it.

CHAPTER THREE

TREATING DEPRESSION

Patients must realize that there are no quick fixes or magic cures for depression, and some people may struggle with it repeatedly over the course of their lifetime. However, the proper therapies and possibly some lifestyle changes will greatly increase a person's chances of successfully achieving and maintaining control over depression. Therapy is generally considered to be the most important aspect of treatment; medication may help control symptoms, but studies have shown that combining medication with therapy produces the best long-term results. Some people's depression may be mild enough to be treated only with therapy.

Seeking a Diagnosis

Experts believe that more than half of all people suffering from depression do not get proper treatment. In many cases, the people who are suffering from depression and their loved ones may not recognize the symptoms. A person may assume that his or her spouse is lazy; a teacher or supervisor at work might think poor concentration is a sign of disinterest; a parent might assume that a child who is acting out is going through a difficult phase. Additionally, people who are suffering from depression often find it difficult to work up the energy to do things that will help them, such as researching therapists or making appointments. "It felt as though the world was

Stigma Surrounding Treatment

Although therapy and medication are extremely helpful tools for many people, society still sometimes attaches a stigma to these treatments. Some people may feel that taking medication is a sign of weakness and refer to it as a "crutch," or something that keeps someone from truly getting over his or her disorder. They may also feel that synthetic, or man-made, medications are bad for the body. However, just as awareness of the symptoms of depression has been growing, awareness of some people's genuine need for medication to control these symptoms has also been growing. When Kristen Bell talked about her decision to start taking antidepressants, she said, "If you do decide to go on a prescription to help yourself, understand that the world wants to shame you for that, but in the medical community, you would never deny a diabetic his insulin … But for some reason, when someone needs a serotonin inhibitor, they're immediately crazy or something."[1]

There is also a stigma surrounding therapy. Some people believe that people who see a therapist are weak, crazy, out of control, spending money unnecessarily, or have no friends. All of these beliefs are false; therapists are professionals who are trained to help people spot unhealthy patterns of behavior and help them think and act in a more positive way. Getting help is a sign of strength, not weakness.

1. Jethro Nededog, "Kristen Bell Says She's Suffered Anxiety and Depression for Years: 'I Fight it All the Time,'" *Business Insider*, May 6, 2016. www.businessinsider.com/kristen-bell-anxiety-and-depression-2016-5.

spinning too fast," said Linda, a 29-year-old woman who was dealing with an ailing mother and a divorce. "I knew there was something wrong, but I barely had enough energy to get out of bed. I just didn't want to deal with anything."[21]

The first step in the treatment of depression, as with any illness, is to recognize the symptoms and seek help from a medical professional. A proper diagnosis is essential for determining the correct treatment, as different types of depression may be treated differently.

Often, the first step in diagnosing depression involves ruling out other illnesses that may have the same symptoms. A physical examination can help a doctor figure out whether the symptoms are caused by a virus or perhaps an enlarged thyroid; lab tests are generally used to measure the level of hormones in the blood and urine as part of this process. Typically, prescription drugs, vitamin supplements, and other medications the patient is taking are reviewed to make sure that the symptoms are not a side effect of a drug or caused by a drug interaction.

A doctor may suggest lab tests to determine whether someone's depression has a medical cause.

Once the doctor has ruled out other possible causes, the patient typically undergoes psychological diagnostic testing. Diagnostic testing is sometimes done by a general practitioner or a mental health professional, such as a psychologist or psychiatrist. Careful analysis of the symptoms, including their onset and severity, can help determine whether depression is the cause. The professional also typically explores the many factors that may put a person at risk for depression, including family history, stress and trauma, medical conditions, alcohol and drug use, and past experience with depressive-type mood disorders.

A thorough diagnostic evaluation also includes a mental health examination to assess the full range of psychological symptoms. This information is used to evaluate the type of depression the person has—whether it is major depression, dysthymia, bipolar disorder, or SAD. The mental health diagnostic information can also be used to help identify any other psychological problems that might be present. The more information that is gathered during the diagnostic process, the better the professional will be able to tailor treatment to the specific needs of the patient.

Diagnostic testing is used to identify and characterize symptoms. In general, the diagnostic criteria for mental disorders fall into one of four categories: affective, behavioral, cognitive, and somatic. Affective, or mood, symptoms may include depressed mood and feelings of worthlessness, hopelessness, or guilt. Behavioral symptoms include agitation and withdrawing from social contact. Cognitive symptoms, or those involving thinking, include poor concentration or indecisiveness. Somatic, or physical, symptoms include changes in sleep or appetite.

Treating Depression with Medication

Once diagnosed, depression can be treated in a number of ways. Generally, the medical doctor or mental health professional will work with the patient to draw up an appropriate treatment plan. Treatment options vary considerably. Factors influencing decisions about appropriate treatment include the type and severity of the depression and its symptoms, as well as individual factors. For instance, meditation and mindfulness work for many people but not for everyone. If the patient has received treatment in the past, the plan will build on what worked; effective therapies used for members of the patient's family might also be included in the treatment plan.

The most common treatments are medication and one of many different types of therapy. The most successful type of therapy for depression is cognitive-behavioral therapy (CBT), which focuses on teaching people how to change their thoughts and behaviors. Experts disagree about whether either of these treatments can be effective on its own. Some doctors prescribe antidepressant drugs without referring patients to therapy, but most professionals warn that drugs do not "cure" the depression; they treat only its symptoms. For this reason, experts caution that therapy is a critical element of treatment. Advocates of therapy believe that it can help people understand the factors that trigger a depressive episode and can help them learn more effective ways of dealing with stress and other problems. For some people, therapy alone is successful treatment, which makes it an attractive option for people who do not want to take antidepressants.

Prescription antidepressant medications are not right for everyone; some people find that they make their symptoms worse, cause suicidal thoughts, or have unpleasant side effects. If this happens, the patient should tell their doctor immediately. Others are opposed to taking synthetic medications and prefer to use natural remedies. However, many people find antidepressants incredibly helpful in controlling their depression. The decision to take or not take medication is a personal one, and the only people who should have a say in it are the patient and their doctors.

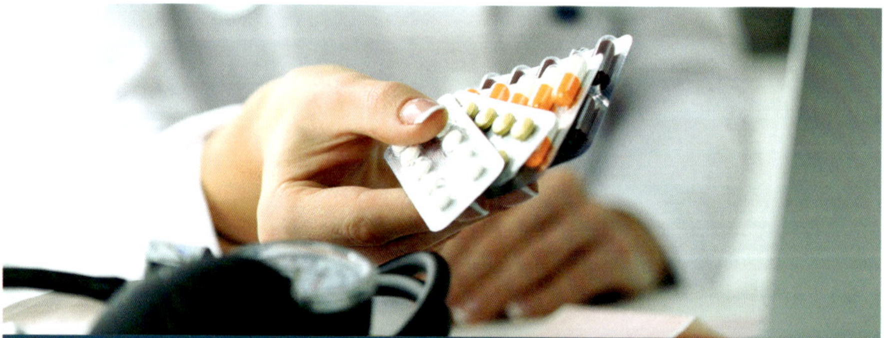

Sometimes patients need to try several different antidepressants before they find one that works for them.

Antidepressants work to normalize the neurotransmitters in the brain that impact mood, notably serotonin, norepinephrine, and dopamine. The most commonly prescribed type of antidepressant medication is selective serotonin reuptake inhibitors (SSRIs). SSRIs increase the level of serotonin by stopping the sending neuron from reabsorbing it. The most widely prescribed SSRIs on the market today include fluoxetine (Prozac), paroxetine (Paxil), and sertraline (Zoloft). The only antidepressants that are currently approved for use in anyone under 18 are Prozac, Zoloft, and Anafranil. Serotonin and norepinephrine reuptake inhibitors (SNRIs) are similar to SSRIs, but they stop the reuptake of norepinephrine as well as serotonin. SNRIs include venlafaxine (Effexor) and duloxetine (Cymbalta). While SSRIs and SNRIs are considered the newest class of antidepressant drugs, some of these drugs have been on the market for more than 20 years. SSRIs quickly became popular because they are effective for a wide variety of symptoms, treat anxiety as well as depression, and tend to have fewer side effects than older classes of antidepressants.

Some patients respond better to other classes of antidepressant drugs, such as monoamine oxidase inhibitors (MAOIs) or tricyclic antidepressants (TCAs). MAOIs work by irreversibly changing the enzyme (monoamine oxidase) that breaks down neurotransmitters so that norepinephrine and serotonin increase in the synapses. MAOIs have proven particularly effective in depression that manifests itself with increased appetite and need for sleep. TCAs, which block the reuptake of norepinephrine into the sending neuron, work well among adult men and in severe cases with many physical symptoms. They are less often used in young or elderly patients because they increase heart rate and lower blood pressure. MAOIs and TCAs are often used as a last resort because of their possible side effects. TCAs and SSRIs share some of the same side effects, such as nausea, drowsiness, dry mouth, and dizziness, but these are generally less severe in SSRIs. With MAOIs, patients must avoid cheeses, pickled foods, chocolates, and alcoholic or nonalcoholic beers or wines because a substance called tryamine will flood the brain. When MAOIs keep monoamine oxidase from doing its job, it cannot mop up the tryamine. Excessive amounts of tryamine can cause blood pressure to rise so severely that blood vessels burst in the brain.

Women who experience depression as a result of PMDD may be prescribed an SSRI to take only during the two weeks before their period, when their PMDD symptoms are present. Although antidepressants typically have to build up in a person's system to have an effect, *Harvard Health Publications* wrote that SSRIs "alleviate PMDD more quickly than depression, which means that women don't necessarily have to take the drugs every day."[22]

Antidepressants do not work the same for every patient, and which drug or combination of drugs will work best in each case is not always clear. For this reason, no one should ever, under any circumstances, take a drug that has been prescribed to a friend or relative, as the results can be unpredictable and

Some drugs have dangerous interactions. A pharmacist can advise patients about which substances to avoid.

dangerous. Additionally, someone who has been prescribed a drug should discuss the side effects and interactions with other drugs with their doctor and pharmacist.

Rarely do antidepressants work immediately. Many patients take the drugs for three to four weeks before they experience the full effect. Patients may have to try different levels of a medication to find the right dosage. It may be tempting for patients to stop taking the antidepressant as their symptoms subside, but doctors warn that symptoms may recur if patients do not take an antidepressant as prescribed.

The risk of addiction to an antidepressant is almost nonexistent, but patients who abruptly stop taking an

The High Cost of Treatment

Although a stigma against medication and therapy does still exist, some surveys have shown that this attitude is slowly changing. According to the *Washington Post*, the ADAA found in 2015 that although only 35 percent of those older than 26 believed seeing a therapist was a sign of strength, that number nearly doubled to 60 percent among people under age 25. The main obstacle for younger people in seeking help is not the fear of what others will think, but the high cost of health insurance.

In the United States, there are many complex factors that go into health insurance prices and coverage, but most people agree that insurance prices are higher than the average American can afford, even if an employer is paying part of the premium (monthly cost). They are higher than in any other developed country in the world, and many insurance plans set limits on what is covered. The lower the monthly premium, the fewer things are covered and the higher the out-of-pocket cost for things that are covered, so someone who chooses a plan with a lower premium may not be paying less in the long term.

Many insurance plans cover prescription medications but do not cover therapy to treat mental illness or stress. Even when they do, many therapists do not accept insurance because they find the insurance system difficult and confusing to manage. For this reason, people may not seek therapy because they are unable to afford it. However, some therapists offer treatment on a sliding scale, meaning that they charge what the client can afford. Many people are advocating for insurance reform so people with mental illnesses will be able to get the help they need.

antidepressant can experience unpleasant withdrawal symptoms. As a result, patients are typically weaned off antidepressants gradually. Generally, a doctor works closely with patients to make sure that stopping a medication does not result in a return of symptoms.

Although studies—and stories from individual patients—seem to support many of the claims of manufacturers and supporters of antidepressant medications, critics say that their supposed benefits may be due to the "placebo effect," which means that the patient feels better simply because he or she thinks that treatment has been provided and not as a result of the medication itself.

Some medical professionals believe that antidepressants are prescribed too often to people suffering "normal" symptoms related to stress or life's difficulties. Experts also caution that antidepressants may not be effective in treating many mild forms of depression. A 2015 study "published in *The Journal of Clinical Psychiatry* reports some 69 percent of people taking selective serotonin reuptake inhibitors (SSRIs), the primary type of antidepressants, have never suffered from major depressive disorder … Today, 11 percent of the American population takes a regular antidepressant, which, by the latest study's measure, may be a severe inflation of what's actually necessary."[23] Critics believe antidepressants have come to be viewed as a quick fix, so people may be unwilling or unable to put in the time and effort of making certain lifestyle changes or attending therapy that may help them deal with negative feelings. Although medication can be highly beneficial to some people, patients should discuss the benefits and drawbacks to medication with their doctor. They may find it helpful to try alternative therapies and only use medication if those do not work. However, this depends on the individual and how severe his or her depression is.

The Role of Therapy

Therapy can play a critical role in treating many forms of depression. Mental health experts emphasize that therapy is particularly important in treatment plans for children and teens. Therapy is generally provided by a psychiatrist or licensed psychologist, social worker, or counselor. Some patients may see improvement in a relatively short period of time, meeting weekly for 10 or 20 weeks; for other patients the therapy may continue much longer. As with other aspects of the treatment plan, this depends on the patient, the type of depression, and the severity of the symptoms.

Therapy is considered an important step in taking control of depression.

The approaches of therapy used to treat depression are many and varied. Generally, they fall into two categories: CBT and interpersonal psychotherapy (IPT). CBT focuses on new ways of thinking to change behavior; the therapist helps patients change negative or unproductive patterns that may contribute to their depression. It is talk therapy based on the theory that people's own ideas, rather than situations or the actions of others, determine the way they think and behave. For instance, if a person's depression causes them to think things such as, "I'm a bad person for being depressed," a therapist can help them change that thought to something positive, such as, "Depression is not my fault and it does not define who I am." It can also help with anxiety, addiction, and other disorders.

IPT helps people understand and work through difficult situations and relationships that may be contributing to their depression. According to experts, "The immediate goals of treatment are rapid symptom reduction and improved social adjustment. The long-term goal is to enable people with depression to make their own needed adjustments. When they can do that, they are better able to cope with and reduce depressive symptoms."[24] IPT has been shown to be especially effective treatment for teens and children. It is a short-term option that is intended to be completed within 12 to 16 weeks.

Many people find that therapy is sufficient to help them overcome their depression, particularly when the symptoms are mild. When a depressive episode is triggered by an external event, for instance, meeting with a mental health professional can help people sort out their feelings and learn how to cope.

Research suggests that patients who rely only on therapy as treatment for major depression may have a greater risk of recurring illness. Still, although experts caution that therapy alone may not work for people with ongoing major depression, some people with lifelong symptoms find that they can wean themselves off antidepressants if they continue therapy treatment.

While meeting one-on-one with a therapist is often highly beneficial, some treatment plans involve the entire family. In this case, the therapist meets with the family to help reduce the stress that may result from having a member with depression, as well as resolve the issues that may be contributing factors to the depression. The therapist can also offer resources to help family members better understand and accept depression as a mental illness, not something that the patient is likely to simply "snap out of." Family therapy may also focus on improving communication and problem-solving skills among family members.

Treatment for Severe Depression

In the mid–20th century, electroconvulsive therapy (ECT)—known then as "shock therapy"—was the main treatment option for severe depression. ECT works by passing electric currents through the brain, deliberately causing a brief seizure. The procedure seems to change brain chemistry, resulting in improved mood, perhaps because it releases so many neurotransmitters simultaneously and speeds up functioning. ECT earned a negative reputation stemming from the early days of its use, when it was administered at high doses without anesthesia. Because of these unsafe practices, ECT remains controversial, even though the treatment today is far different. According to NAMI, ECT is safer than it was in the 1940s—today, patients are asleep during the procedure and are able to go about their normal tasks about an hour after they wake up—but it still has a number of risks and side effects. These include confusion, "headaches, muscle pain, nausea," and "memory loss, which can range from forgetting conversations or events right before and after a treatment, forgetting things from weeks or months before treatment, and less commonly, from years before."[25]

ECT is generally reserved for cases of severe depression accompanied by delusions or hallucinations or in which the person has suicidal or homicidal thoughts or urges. ECT may also be used when a patient with severe depression cannot take antidepressants or has not responded to other treatment options. An estimated 100,000 people worldwide receive ECT every year, generally in a course of 6 to 12 treatments administered 2 or 3 times a week for about a month.

This image shows what a patient looks like during ECT.

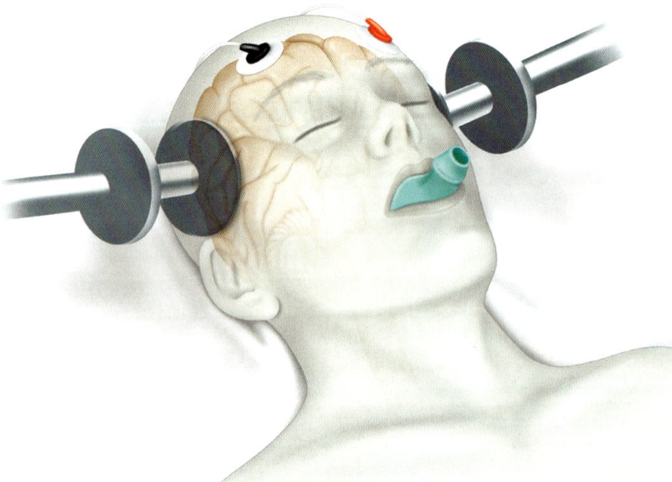

One of the advantages of ECT over antidepressants is that it typically works much more rapidly. Some patients need only one course of ECT before they feel its benefit. Others may need several courses of ECT over a year or so. Patients undergoing ECT often are prescribed an antidepressant or mood stabilizing medication to prevent relapse after ECT. Julie K. Hersh, author of the book *Struck by Living: From Depression to Hope*, wrote in *Psychology Today*,

> *Most ECT success stories never hit the news. Understandably, people benefiting from ECT want normalcy, without the label of mental illness. ECT is often used in critical situations, in an effort to avoid suicide. I know from personal experience. After three suicide attempts, ECT provided a quick and clear path out of my depression.*[26]

Using Light to Treat SAD

Special lamps have been developed to treat SAD and some other types of depression by exposure to bright artificial light. They are called light boxes or sun lamps, and they mimic natural daylight. Daily exposure to the light is thought to alter or reestablish the body's natural, healthy sleep-wake cycle and suppress the release of melatonin. Together, these factors cause biochemical changes in the brain that may help reduce or control symptoms of depression.

According to Anne Shea, a 28-year-old from Pittsburgh,

> *I have had SAD for as long as I can remember. When winter drags on and every day is gray and cold, it's hard to remember it will ever get warm and sunny again. On those days, it's hard to get out of my bed in the morning. A few years ago, I got a "Happy Light" for my desk. The full spectrum light is meant to mimic the mood-boosting, fatigue-zapping powers of the summer sun. I was skeptical, but my Happy Light actually helps me get through the worst of it, especially when I hit my usual midday slump. It's like a nice little boost of energy on my hardest days.*[27]

Sun lamps offer an inexpensive and convenient means of treatment with very few side effects. They are often used together with medication, psychotherapy, or other treatment approaches.

Sun lamps can help improve the symptoms of SAD.

A Natural Approach

A number of herbs and alternative medicines have been proposed to treat depression. The most widely used herb is the extract from St. John's wort, a wildflower considered a weed in most of the United States. Its reputation for improving the symptoms of depression, anxiety, and several other mood disorders has made St. John's wort one of the best-selling botanical extracts in the United States.

More than 30 clinical studies have been conducted over the past 25 years to evaluate the effectiveness of St. John's wort. Results have been mixed. While some scientific evidence suggests that St. John's wort is helpful in treating mild to moderate depression, two large studies sponsored by the National Center for Complementary and Alternative Medicine (NCCAM) showed that the herb was no more effective than a placebo in treating major depression of moderate severity.

Other remedies suggested by advocates of alternative medicine include S-adenosylmethionine (SAM-e), an amino acid believed to improve brain chemistry; 5-hydroxytryptophan (5-HTP), an amino acid that is converted by the brain to serotonin; L-theanine, an amino acid found in green tea that has been shown to create a sense of relaxation; and fish oil capsules, which contain two brain chemicals: eicosapentaenoic acid (EPA) and docosahexaenoic acid (DHA). People with depression may have low levels of these chemicals.

Green tea contains an amino acid that may help lessen the symptoms of depression.

For some people, these remedies are useful in relieving the symptoms of depression, but it is important to recognize that herbs are sold as food, not drugs, and are not regulated by the U.S. Food and Drug Administration (FDA). In addition, sellers of herbal remedies are not required to list warnings of side effects. Experts caution that the placebo effect may account for many of the benefits people claim they have experienced from these alternative remedies.

Herbal remedies for depression can be dangerous. Research has shown that St. John's wort, for instance, can have serious negative side effects and adverse drug interactions. The FDA cautions that the herb appears to interfere with certain medications used to treat heart disease, depression, and seizures; it can also decrease the effectiveness of birth control pills. Because 5-HTP releases serotonin, taking it with other antidepressants can lead to a potentially life-threatening adverse drug reaction called "serotonin syndrome," which is when too much serotonin floods the brain.

Finding the Right Treatment Plan

Not all treatment options are equal. People react uniquely to different drugs, different therapists, and different approaches. Moreover, some medications that appear to work well at the outset of treatment may lose effectiveness. Regardless of the treatment plan, recovery often depends upon ongoing monitoring so that the doctor and patient can change the course of treatment if it is not working.

Finding the right therapist can be especially tricky. Sometimes people need to go to three or four people before they find the one who is the right fit for them. It is perfectly acceptable for someone to choose a different therapist whose personality and approach to the problem fits with the patient's wants and needs. For example, some patients may want to joke around about their problems, while others want to speak about them very seriously. Finding a therapist who can match the patient's tone is very important in this case. It is up to the patient to do research, ask questions, and trust their instincts when it comes to finding a therapist. Finding the right person may be a stressful and time-consuming task, but therapy is no use if the patient is not comfortable with the person he or she is working with. Therefore, it is well worth the effort. Asking a friend or trusted adult to help may make the process easier.

Many people who are treated for a depressive episode go on to live healthy lives without a recurrence. This is particularly true when a depressive episode is triggered by a specific circumstance. Women with postpartum depression, for instance, typically feel better after a few months, after they have adjusted to their new life and their hormones are back to normal. Similarly, people who suffer a depressive episode triggered by a major life change may be able to be weaned off of antidepressants as they adjust to the change.

Depression may seem like it will last forever, but it can be overcome.

For some people with depression, the illness may be a lifelong condition with symptoms that ebb and flow. Hopelessness is common when people are at the darkest depths of depression, but many highly successful people in all walks of life have struggled—and continue to struggle—with the disease. People who have experienced episodes of major depression often learn to recognize the stressors that trigger their depression and how to avoid or cope with such stressors. People with depression also learn to recognize the symptoms of their illness and to seek treatment early on, before the depression becomes serious. They may take antidepressants; go to therapy; or use exercise, diet, or meditation to fight off the symptoms of depressive illness.

CHAPTER FOUR

TAKING CONTROL OF DEPRESSION

When people are at their lowest point, they may feel as if depression is a life sentence. However, there are many things someone with depression can do to make themselves feel better. Some may struggle with periods of depression throughout their life; at these times, it is important for them to be compassionate with themselves and understand that there is nothing wrong with them.

In the deepest periods of depression, people may feel a sense of hopelessness and dread, but those who have recovered are quick to share with others what helped them emerge from their darkest despair and what continues to help them stay one step ahead of the illness. For instance, actress Carrie Fisher, who is best known for her role as Leia in the Star Wars movies, was always outspoken about her struggle with bipolar disorder and how she coped with it. She was especially vocal about how ECT had helped her, which went a long way toward changing the way people viewed it: no longer as a frightening, dangerous procedure, but as one of the most effective treatments for severe depression that is difficult or impossible to control through medication.

Trying Different Options

Many people diagnosed with depression have felt sad for years without knowing why. A diagnosis of depression is often a relief, although no cure has been found, and treatment generally does not have an immediate effect on symptoms. Some patients do not respond well to their prescribed medication. Sometimes it takes weeks or months to find the best drug or combination of drugs.

The search for the correct combination of drugs can be frustrating, but patients who have been helped by prescription drugs encourage those who do not respond to a drug right away to keep looking for a solution. Different classes of drugs work differently. One patient said she tried many prescription drugs during her 10-year battle with depression. She encouraged others to continue to work with their doctors to find the optimal solution. "Try the SNRI medications if you have not already," she wrote. "Compare them with how you felt on strictly SSRIs. You may learn something about your own brain chemistry that can help you select the right anti-depressant to defeat your depression once and for all. I know this information has helped me combat mine … Since being on [an SNRI], I feel happier than I have in years."[28]

Supporting Someone with Depression

Depression affects everyone who suffers from it in different ways. The symptoms can range from mild to severe, and not everyone has the same ones. Some people cry for seemingly no reason, while others feel numb and display no emotion. Additionally, people's responses to certain words or actions can vary. For instance, one person may feel better when they receive hugs and attention, while another may simply want to be left alone.

Depression can be difficult and frustrating for loved ones to deal with, especially if the sufferer cannot or will not take steps to get treatment. Parents may get annoyed with a child who does not have enough energy to keep his or her room clean, and friends may find it difficult to relate to someone who has suddenly become more negative and socially isolated. However, a strong support network is important in helping people with depression feel less despairing and more able to take steps to help themselves. It is important for friends and relatives to let someone with depression know that they are there to listen and help.

People with depression often feel guilty for how their feelings affect others, so loved ones can help by reassuring the sufferer that they are still loved. They should not reinforce the person's guilt; instead, they should validate their feelings by saying things such as, "I understand why you feel frustrated and I'm sorry you're dealing with this." Rather than assuming what someone needs, they should ask what they can do to help. The person may want help finding a therapist, distractions to help them feel better, or simply a listening ear and a shoulder to cry on.

A strong support network makes it easier for someone to deal with depression.

Although offering support is important, loved ones should remember that they also need to take care of their own mental health. Writer Wiley Reading offered this advice:

> *Imagine for a moment hearing "you're too much for me" from every single loved one in your life. That's what depression does to you. It makes you feel like*

a burden to the world. This doesn't mean that you need to be a constant source of emotional support for a depressed person. It's not your job to take care of anyone's mental health. *A good way to take care of yourself without sending your depressed loved one spiraling is to say things like "I need not to be the only one you talk to about this stuff" or to address specific behaviors that you would like them to stop or change … Don't act like they need to try to find positivity where there is none. Tell them* you *need positivity so you'd like to talk about something positive, even if they don't have anything positive going on. And if they absolutely can't redirect, take a break to surround yourself in the positivity you need and come back later.*[29]

Personal Responsibility

As patients with depression await a treatment that will help them function, they sometimes no longer find the energy or desire to continue their normal activities. They may drop out of school, stop going to work, or find a less demanding job. When they do not have the energy for or interest in activities, their relationships with others might deteriorate and friendships might erode. In short, people may find themselves with a diminishing quality of life.

Family members and friends often agree that living with someone with depression can be difficult. In many people, the depression manifests itself as moodiness, irritability, forgetfulness, and anxiety. A person with depression may be unpredictable and prone to emotional outbursts of anger or tears. Family members and friends who do not understand that these are symptoms of depression might take the outbursts personally and respond with anger. Even those who know a loved one has depression might not know what to do or say. Some people choose to say nothing rather than risk saying the wrong things. Better education about depression and its physical causes can help reduce the stigma and build bridges between a person with depression and his or her loved ones.

However, although depression is a mental illness whose effects on the brain and body cannot be controlled through sheer willpower, it is important to remember that having this disorder does not excuse poor behavior. It is not fair to anyone involved to dismiss hurtful words and actions by blaming the disorder. It makes friends and family feel upset and guilty, and it creates a sense of powerlessness for the person with the disorder. Feeling constantly out of control of their actions can increase the negative emotions depression sufferers feel as a result of their illness, but knowing that they do have control over how they react to their illness can give them a sense of empowerment.

Many people feel that responsibility is the same thing as blame, but this is not true. People with any kind of mental disorder are not to blame for their feelings, but if their words or actions are hurtful to others, they should try to make amends. For instance, if someone's depression makes them feel irritable and they say something harsh to a loved one, they should apologize when they feel calmer. They should not tell the person, "I don't owe you an apology because my depression makes me irritable and therefore I can't be held accountable for anything I say."

Depression in Young People

Mental health experts say that treating depression can be particularly challenging when the patient is a child or teenager. First, it is more difficult to diagnose depression in children because many of the symptoms of depression—changes in appetite, moodiness, temper tantrums—are typical of a normal, healthy childhood. In adolescence, too, it can be difficult to tell that something is wrong. Teenagers often sleep late,

The Benefits of Humor

Many people with depression find that humor helps them cope with their feelings. Numerous studies have found that laughing releases stress-reducing hormones and helps people bond. According to laughter consultant Joe Bluett:

> *Laughter has a way of instantly connecting people and is one of the most basic and fundamental ways in which we communicate as human beings. But more than that—laughter can increase confidence, self-esteem, creativity, positivity and resilience, bringing positive changes to all aspects of our lives. A number of my laughter club regulars have embraced huge positive changes in their lives—eg losing weight, returning to work after years of illness and/or depression; coping with serious health diagnosis and grief; coping with the isolation and stress of being a full time carer.*[1]

Laughter consultants are mental health professionals who use humor to help people overcome their stress and symptoms of mental illness. They may lead laughter yoga groups, where people alternate laughing for no reason with breathing exercises. People who are not willing or able to join one of these groups may find it helpful to watch a comedy show or read a funny book.

Laughter has been proven to have numerous health benefits.

1. Quoted in Ryan Barrell, "How Laughter and Comedy Can Help with Depression, Anxiety and Other Mental Illnesses," *Huffington Post*, January 7, 2016. www.huffingtonpost.co.uk/entry/the-best-medicine_uk_57702a73e4b0232d331e3262.

experience changes in appetite, and appear withdrawn, aloof, or emotional.

However, experts stress the importance of early diagnosis and treatment of depression in young people. Left untreated, teen depression can lead to problems at home and school, drug abuse, self-hatred, risky behavior, and even suicide. Unlike adults, children and teenagers generally depend on parents and other caregivers to get them the help they need.

Because it can be hard for parents to recognize the signs of depression in young adults, teens who feel they are depressed or going through a harder time than normal should have a conversation with their parents about their feelings. This can be difficult, especially if the teen's depression has been causing tension within the family. Starting the conversation with an apology for past behavior may be a good way to make parents more receptive to hearing what the teen has to say.

It can be helpful for teens to write down what they want to say before they ask their parents to talk. Clinical psychologist and adolescent specialist Jerry Weichman suggested printing out a list of symptoms and highlighting the ones the person is experiencing so their parents can see they are dealing with more than just normal teen emotions. The conversation should take place when no one is upset or busy. However, even in the best circumstances, parents might find it difficult to understand at first. The following are some tips for dealing with different negative reactions:

- ***Guilt-tripping.*** *Your parents might say something like, "You have the best life! You have a roof over your head/lots of friends/whatever. You shouldn't be depressed!" If they do, respond with, "Yeah, you're right. I agree. I shouldn't be feeling this way, and that's how I know I need help."*

- ***Minimizing the situation.*** *They might say, "All teenagers are moody sometimes. You're just having a bad day. Stress is normal!" In which case, you can respond with something like, "I understand what you're saying, but this is more than that. This is having an impact on me and my ability to live my life. I don't know how to manage it on my own and I need help."*

- ***Making it about them.*** *Think, "I failed, I'm such a bad parent, I can't even raise a kid who is happy." In this case, you can say something like, "It's not that you're not doing enough. I'm not saying that anything in our family or my school or our environment needs to change, it's that I need help."*[30]

Why Is Teen Depression on the Rise?

There are many theories about why teens seem to be experiencing more depression and anxiety than previous generations. Some people believe it is simply that more teens are seeking help. Others feel it is because parents tend to try to protect their children more than previous generations did, leading young adults to be spoiled and have a harder time dealing with things. However, some experts believe changes in society may be a large factor:

> *They are the post-9/11 generation, raised in an era of economic and national insecurity. They've never known a time when terrorism and school shootings weren't the norm. They grew up watching their parents weather a severe recession, and, perhaps most important, they hit puberty at a time when technology and social media were transforming society … Every fight or slight is documented online for hours or days after the incident. It's exhausting …*
>
> *Steve Schneider, a counselor at Sheboygan South High School in southeastern Wisconsin, says the situation is like a scab that's constantly being picked. "At no point do you get to remove yourself from it and get perspective," he says. It's hard for many adults to understand how much of teenagers' emotional life is lived within the small screens of their phones, but a CNN special report in 2015 conducted with researchers at the University of California, Davis, and the University of Texas at Dallas examined the social-media use of more than 200 13-year-olds. Their analysis found that "there is no firm line between their real and online worlds," according to the researchers.*[1]

Although teens' phones and the Internet can be useful tools in helping them stay connected with friends and do research for school, they may benefit from taking periodic breaks from technology. Additionally, researchers found that pressure to do well in school was an important factor in the increase of anxiety and depression. Teens may find it helpful to speak to their parents or a counselor who can help them find ways to reduce the amount of stress they are under at school.

1. Susanna Schrobsdorff, "Teen Depression and Anxiety: Why the Kids Are Not Alright," *TIME*, October 27, 2016. time.com/4547322/american-teens-anxious-depressed-overwhelmed/.

If talking to their parents face-to-face seems too overwhelming, teens can write a letter or ask another trusted adult, such as a school guidance counselor or their pediatrician, to be there for the conversation.

Ways to Deal with Depression

Outside of medical treatment, having a strong network of family and friends is perhaps the most important predictor of whether a person will recover from depression and its symptoms. Fortunately, many support groups can help people with depression as well as their families. Support groups share information about the disorder and offer personal insight into treatment options and coping techniques. Some depression support groups are sponsored by nonprofit health care organizations or local government agencies; others meet informally.

Support groups that meet over the Internet may be particularly helpful to people with severe depression or who fear a new situation. Internet support groups also have the advantage of allowing people to stay anonymous, which may help those who worry about the stigma of mental illness. For some people, local groups that enable people with depression to make connections with one another and reduce the sense of isolation may be important aspects of a treatment plan. Support groups also can help family members adjust to a loved one's depression.

Some experts say that maintaining a positive attitude is the most important thing people can do. Individuals who are depressed are not likely to "snap out of it," but therapists say such people can take steps to convince themselves that they feel better. People who are severely depressed might need to set small, realistic goals for themselves, such as getting out of bed or bathing. Other goals might focus on activities the person used to enjoy, such as seeing a friend or going to a movie, ballgame, or other event. One of the dangers of depression is the isolation that results; experts emphasize the importance of maintaining relationships with others.

People who are depressed may find themselves spending more time alone, which can make depression worse.

Depression saps a person's energy. For this reason, it is important to break up large tasks into small ones and to set priorities to experience a sense of accomplishment. Experts also emphasize the importance of being nice to oneself.

Many people believe that the best treatment for depression is a healthy lifestyle. A well-balanced diet and moderate daily exercise can help prevent a depressive state from deepening. Making lifestyle changes and adopting a healthy regime can be a crucial part of treatment.

Most experts recommend regular exercise as a treatment for depression, even if the person is already taking medication and going to therapy. Exercise boosts endorphins, which are brain chemicals that improve mood. In addition, physical activity burns up stress chemicals such as adrenaline and promotes a more relaxed state of mind.

Research suggests that even moderate exercise can help in mild to moderate cases of depression. "I chose to cease SSRI medication four years ago and rely upon [other] strategies to maintain my wellness," wrote one depression patient. "In my case, the benefits of a daily 30-40 minute [exercise] session within an hour of waking have been measurable, including an increase of energy, elevated mood, and motivation."[31]

In a 2006 study conducted by researchers from the University of Texas, for instance, moderate physical activity such as a brisk 30-minute walk was shown to ease depressive symptoms. Although the effect was almost immediate, researchers are quick to emphasize that exercise is a short-term solution for the symptoms of depression, not a cure for the disease itself.

Aside from the physical impact on depression, exercise may benefit patients in other ways. Some forms of exercise may serve as a social event. Participating in a weekly exercise class or joining a team sport might help reduce feelings of isolation. An enjoyable period of exercise might be distracting enough to break the vicious cycle of pessimistic thinking, and simply taking a more active role in one's own recovery can be a boost to self-esteem.

Exercising with other people may have a double benefit for depression sufferers because both exercise and socialization can improve a person's mood.

The Benefits of a Healthy Diet

Vitamin deficiencies may contribute to symptoms associated with depression. For instance, the B-complex vitamins are essential to mental and emotional well-being. The body cannot store them, so people depend entirely on their daily diets for an adequate supply. In addition, B vitamins are destroyed by things such as caffeine, sugar, alcohol, and nicotine. Some people who experience anxiety, stress, or other symptoms associated with depression try to relax with a cigarette, binge on food, or self-medicate with alcohol, so it is no surprise that many people with depression may be deficient in B vitamins.

Meditation and Yoga

Although they do not work for every person, many people find that meditation and yoga ease feelings of stress and increase feelings of well-being. The *New York Times* explained that the effects of meditation and exercise can be seen in the brain:

> *As many people know from experience, depression is characterized in part by an inability to stop dwelling on gloomy thoughts and unhappy memories from the past. Researchers suspect that this thinking pattern, known as rumination, may involve two areas of the brain in particular: the prefrontal cortex, a part of the brain that helps to control attention and focus, and the hippocampus, which is critical for learning and memory. In some studies, people with severe depression have been found to have a smaller hippocampus than people who are not depressed.*
>
> *Interestingly, meditation and exercise affect those same portions of the brain, although in varying ways. In brain-scan studies, people who are long-term meditators, for instance, generally display different patterns of brain-cell communication in their prefrontal cortex during cognitive tests than people who don't meditate. Those differences are believed to indicate that the meditators possess a more honed ability to focus and concentrate … attributes that are believed to help reduce stubborn rumination.*[1]

1. Gretchen Reynolds, "Meditation Plus Running as a Treatment for Depression," *New York Times* Well Blog, March 16, 2016. well.blogs.nytimes.com/2016/03/16/meditation-plus-running-as-a-treatment-for-depression/.

Similarly, deficiencies in a number of minerals, including magnesium, zinc, iron, and potassium, can cause exhaustion, lethargy, and lack of appetite. A calcium deficiency has been shown to affect the central nervous system, causing nervousness, apprehension, irritability, and numbness. For these reasons, many experts believe that a properly balanced diet may be a key element of a depression treatment plan.

It is also important for patients to eat enough protein to maintain skin, organ, muscle, and immune function. Recent research suggests that one particular component of protein, the amino acid tryptophan, is important in its effect on the brain, where it influences mood. Tryptophan can be added to the diet by ensuring that at least one type of protein is eaten at each meal. These include fish, meat, eggs, milk, cheese, nuts, beans, lentils, or tofu.

A healthy diet can help reduce depression.

Experts also emphasize the importance of sleep. In fact, some studies show that inadequate sleep may cause depression. Learning stress reduction techniques may be helpful in reducing depression. Some people find yoga, meditation, and breathing techniques helpful. These strategies date back to ancient Asian philosophies and help people focus on the present moment. Therapists working with patients with depression sometimes use meditation or relaxation techniques to help patients change the way they react to situations and manage their feelings. These techniques can help relieve stress by helping people accept what cannot be changed.

Stability is important. Establishing a routine will enable people with depression to learn what works for them, how they can minimize the symptoms of the illness, and how to recognize the warning signs that a depressive episode is getting worse. The path to recovery requires patients to keep appointments with their doctors and other mental health professionals, follow their doctors' advice, and take medications as prescribed. It also requires patients to be willing to talk about their moods and feelings. Building a support network of family, friends, and others who understand what patients with depression are going through is critical. Some people also find that taking notes on what is happening at school or work, as well as on sleep, eating, and exercise patterns, can help identify stressors that may trigger or increase depressive symptoms. Finally, education is important because it allows patients to make informed decisions about treatment and to feel as much in control as possible of their depression and its symptoms.

CHAPTER FIVE

LEARNING MORE ABOUT DEPRESSION

Experts' understanding of depression has come a long way in the last several decades, but there is still much they do not know. The exact causes of depression are still unknown, which means experimentation with several different treatments is necessary. Research into depression is ongoing, and new things are being discovered all the time that can help medical professionals create the most effective treatment plan for their patients.

In addition to helping develop treatment plans, research into the causes of depression can help with refining the diagnosis. Many experts believe that depression is overdiagnosed in today's society. *The Atlantic* reported a study by Ramin Mojtabai of the Johns Hopkins Bloomberg School of Public Health. He used face-to-face interviews to reevaluate 5,639 participants who had been diagnosed with depression by a doctor outside of a hospital between 2009 and 2010. The results found that only "38.4 percent of participants who had been diagnosed with depression by their doctor were judged in the [reevaluation] to have had a major depressive episode in the past year."[32] However, the majority of participants, even those who did not meet the criteria for any kind of depression, reported using antidepressants. A clearer understanding of what is considered depression can help determine whether antidepressants are truly necessary for a patient.

A Better Diagnosis

Although depression is a real disorder that can be debilitating, it can sometimes be difficult for doctors to know when someone has it. Depression-like symptoms are common in people who have been through a stressful experience such as a divorce or natural disaster. Some scientists warn that antidepressant drugs are being used to treat these symptoms, which are in fact natural or normal reactions to stress. Jerome Wakefield, who led a 2007 study of depression, warned that using a checklist of symptoms to diagnose depression is insufficient and that doctors do not pay enough attention to the circumstances involved. "The cost of not looking at context is you think anyone who comes under this diagnosis has a biological disorder, so should more or less automatically get antidepressant medication, and everything else is superfluous," Wakefield said. "There is a trend to treat people in this somewhat mechanized way."[33] Several studies are looking at improving the diagnostic tools used by professionals to add components that would help differentiate between people who are reacting to stress and those who are truly depressed.

In the future, scientists might be able to use MRIs and other imaging methods as diagnostic tools for depression. Early studies comparing the brain of a person with depression to that of a person without depression suggest that there are important differences. For instance, the hippocampus, which regulates emotion and memory, of patients with depression tends to be smaller. In addition, images of the brains of bipolar patients show an unusual number of bright spots in some of the regions involved in mood, including the thalamus, basal ganglia, and brain stem. One recent study suggested that increased activity in the amygdala of the left hemisphere might indicate heightened vulnerability to future depression.

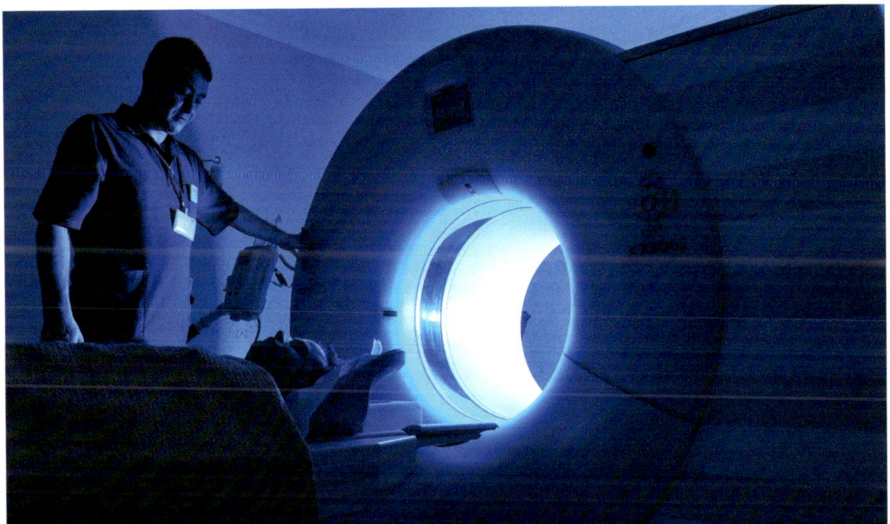

Researchers are using MRIs to learn more about how the brains of people with depression compare to those of people without depression.

Improvements in imaging technology might also make it possible to examine the concentrations of neurotransmitters, so that densities of those molecules can be compared in different people and in various areas of the brain.

Researchers are especially concerned about improving diagnostic techniques for the elderly, children, and adolescents. Symptoms of depression among the elderly are often believed to be signs of aging or mistaken for dementia. In children and teens, the symptoms can resemble attention-deficit hyperactivity disorder (ADHD) or other illnesses, or they may be overlooked as a normal part of adolescence. Studies that use high-tech imaging to identify brain activity may eventually help distinguish depression from other ailments, enabling quicker, more accurate diagnoses for at-risk populations. However, as of right now, the technology is not able to detect multiple disorders with accuracy. Since many people struggle with more than one mental illness—for example, anxiety and depression—more accurate results are achieved when a doctor makes a diagnosis, rather than a machine.

What Is an MRI?

Scientists are comparing the brains of people with and without depression to learn whether differences in the structure of the brain might be a contributing factor to depression. Many of these studies rely on brain-imaging technologies.

One of the technologies often used to study the brain is MRI. The MRI machine is essentially a giant scanner. A horizontal tube runs through the machine from front to back. The patient, lying on his or her back, slides into the tube. The scan uses a magnetic field with radio wave pulses of energy to build a map of tissue types. It then integrates this information into a 2-D or 3-D image of the human brain.

Understanding the Causes of Depression

Researchers are investigating the many causes of depression in an effort to determine how the contributing factors interrelate. According to *Harvard Health Publications*, "Research suggests that depression doesn't spring from simply having too much or too little of certain brain chemicals. Rather, depression has many possible causes, including faulty mood regulation by the brain, genetic vulnerability, stressful life events, medications, and medical problems. It's believed that several of these forces interact to bring on depression."[34]

One theory for the causes of SAD and bipolar disorder is irregularity in circadian rhythms—the body's internal clock that determines when people wake and sleep. Most people's body clock regulates itself, but in some people, especially those with SAD, the clock can be disrupted. Some researchers believe circadian rhythms "can be thrown off by the late dawn and early dusk of winter."[35] Exposing SAD patients to a sun lamp may help reset the body's clock and improve mood.

Scientists are also looking at how life events, stress, thought patterns, and personality affect the onset of depression. Looking at family histories and the pattern that depression takes in one individual's life can help researchers better understand the factors that might lead to recurring episodes.

Researchers would also like to learn more about the role that sexual, physical, and emotional abuse plays in depression. Studies suggest a link between childhood abuse and neglect and adult depression. One recent study compared the experience of patients who had suffered abuse as children with those who had not. The study found that those who had been abused as children tended to become depressed at a younger age, have more severe symptoms, were more likely to self-medicate through drugs and alcohol, and were more likely to attempt suicide.

The role of genetics is also the subject of a great deal of research. Scientists believe that a genetic component contributes to depression and are conducting research to identify the gene or genes that may carry the disease. Some researchers are studying the deoxyribonucleic acid (DNA) of people in families with two or more members who have depression in an attempt to figure out which gene or genes might make people more susceptible to the disease and its symptoms.

Scientists are currently studying the role DNA plays in depression.

Some scientists are studying the impact of a gene called corticotropin-releasing hormone receptor one (CRHR1), which controls the body's response to stress hormones. In one recent study of people who had suffered child abuse, those who carried the most protective form of the gene had markedly lower measures of depression.

Some medical conditions are associated with depression, but researchers are unsure whether the disease itself causes changes in the brain that lead to depression or whether it is simply the stress of having a medical condition that leads someone to become depressed. For instance, someone who has cancer may develop depression due to the fear of dying, financial worries caused by high hospital bills, and the stress of receiving chemotherapy or radiation treatment.

Research through NIMH

NIMH is one of the world's leading mental health biomedical organizations. The mission of NIMH is to transform the understanding and treatment of mental illnesses through basic and clinical research, paving the way for prevention, recovery, and cure.

NIMH researchers are involved in a wide range of studies on the causes, diagnosis, prevention, and treatment of depression in the United States. Some of this research is done in-house, but NIMH also provides grants to support research at universities, hospitals, and other research institutions throughout the United States and the world.

NIMH is working with scientists in different disciplines to use the tools of molecular and cellular biology, genetics, epidemiology, and cognitive and behavioral science to better understand the factors that influence brain function and behavior, including mental illness. It is particularly focused on research that will help scientists work together to translate research in the laboratory to real-world uses.

New Treatment Options

Much of the research on depression focuses on treatment options. Of particular concern to many researchers is the treatment of depression in children and teens. Experts have long believed that successfully addressing depression in young people may be the key to avoiding later serious bouts of the illness. In addition, interest in addressing depression among young people has also grown in response to serious concerns about prescribing antidepressants to young people. Closely monitored clinical trials are being undertaken to explore the link between antidepressants and suicidal thoughts in teens. There are also studies being conducted on how antidepressant medications affect the developing brain in the hope of developing safer options for teenage patients. Researchers are exploring some of the differences between teens and adults to learn more about how to craft treatment plans that address the specific needs of teens. They are especially concerned about teens' higher risk of suicide and their inability to seek treatment on their own due to age, transportation, and financial restrictions. Additionally, they are also are looking at the long-term effectiveness of psychotherapy and medication on teen depression and on the factors that influence recovery.

A number of newer, non-antidepressant treatment options are available as well. One such treatment, called transcranial magnetic stimulation, or TMS, involves applying powerful electromagnets directly to the skull. TMS is based on the realization that electrical activity in the part of the brain that is believed to control mood is diminished in depressed patients. TMS uses electromagnets to send pulses of energy directly into this part of the brain, creating an electric current and getting the brain cells to fire. "One can think of this as sort of getting a jumper cable and jump-starting your car because your battery has been drained,"[36] said neurologist Alvaro Pascual-Leone, who has used TMS at Beth Israel Deaconess Medical Center in Boston. According to NAMI, "The doctor performing the treatment will determine the amount of magnetic energy needed during the first treatment session. TMS treatments will last about 40 minutes. Unlike ECT, TMS does not require the use of anesthesia and [the] person will remain awake during the treatment."[37] Side effects include muscle contractions, headaches, and seizures if the person has a history of them.

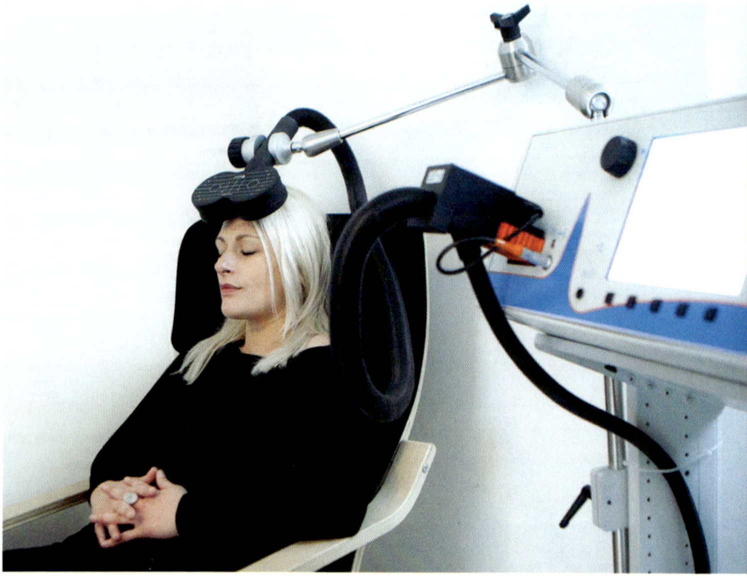

TMS is a treatment therapy for severe depression involving powerful magnets.

Antidepressants such as Prozac and Paxil have made pharmaceutical companies billions of dollars, so it is no surprise that drug companies are constantly involved in researching potential drugs. Drug testing is a long process, however. Chemical compounds are first tried in a lab and then tested on animals. Only after years of testing to ensure that a potential remedy is safe can it be used on people in clinical trials.

One drug that is currently being studied is ketamine, which is currently used mainly by veterinarians as a tranquilizer. In 2016, researchers found that in mice, a substance that is produced when ketamine breaks down in the body can lift depression in hours or even minutes, which is much faster than the current antidepressant drugs on the market. Further research must be done to see if this substance works the same way in humans. Clinical trials on humans, in which very low doses of the drug are administered through an IV drip, have been mixed; ketamine works quickly and treats severe depression, but people often relapse about a week after receiving a treatment. Additionally, "despite legitimate medical uses, ketamine also has dissociative, euphoric, and addictive properties, making it a potential drug of abuse and limiting its usefulness as a depression medication."[38] Researchers caution that ketamine should only be used to treat depression under the strict supervision of a doctor.

Looking toward the Future

With advancing technology and new research into the causes and treatment of depression, medical professionals hope to be able to help people find relief more quickly and effectively. However, as of right now, there is no proven cure for depression. Treatment takes hard work and dedication, but the majority of people say the results are worth it.

Although researchers do not know exactly what combination of factors causes depression, they do know it is not the fault of the person suffering from this disorder. People with depression do not enjoy the way they feel or the way the disorder affects their lives, and if they could simply make a decision to feel better, they would. Therapy and medication can be effective treatments, but they take time to work. People can help a loved one with depression by being understanding and compassionate. Changing the way society views depression and other mental illnesses is another important step toward improving the recovery process.

NOTES

Introduction: More Than Just Sadness

1. Criss, "How Does Depression Affect Your Daily Life?," Depression-Guide.com. www.depression-guide.com/depression-affect.htm.
2. "Depression," Anxiety and Depression Association of America. www.adaa.org/understanding-anxiety/depression.

Chapter One: Defining Depression

3. Quoted in Madeline Boardman, "Jared Padalecki Reveals Struggle with Depression: 'There's No Shame,'" *Us Weekly*, March 13, 2015. www.usmagazine.com/celebrity-news/news/jared-padalecki-reveals-depression-struggle-theres-no-shame-2015133.
4. Mayo Clinic Staff, "Persistent Depressive Disorder (Dysthymia)," Mayo Clinic, December 19, 2015. www.mayoclinic.org/diseases-conditions/persistent-depressive-disorder/symptoms-causes/dxc-20166596.
5. Virginia Edwards, *Depression and Bipolar Disorders: Everything You Need to Know*. Richmond Hill, ON: Firefly, 2002, p. 21.
6. Chrissy Teigen, "Chrissy Teigen Opens Up for the First Time About Her Postpartum Depression," *Glamour*, March 6, 2017. www.glamour.com/story/chrissy-teigen-postpartum-depression.
7. Teigen, "Chrissy Teigen Opens Up."
8. Teigen, "Chrissy Teigen Opens Up."

9. "What Bipolar Disorder Feels Like," Bipolar Disorder Today. www.mental-health-today.com/bp/art11.htm.

10. Mayo Clinic Staff, "Depression (Major Depressive Disorder): Risk Factors," Mayo Clinic, July 7, 2016. www.mayoclinic.org/diseases-conditions/depression/basics/risk-factors/con-20032977.

11. "Major Depression Among Adolescents," National Institute of Mental Health. www.nimh.nih.gov/health/statistics/prevalence/major-depression-among-adolescents.shtml.

12. Barbara Greenberg, Ph.D., "Why Are So Many Teen Girls Depressed?," *Psychology Today*, July 30, 2012. www.psychologytoday.com/blog/the-teen-doctor/201207/why-are-so-many-teen-girls-depressed.

13. Megan Gannon, "Depression Doubles Missed Work Days," LiveScience, July 24, 2013. www.livescience.com/38403-depression-doubles-missed-work-days.html.

Chapter Two: The Truth about Depression

14. "Biological Causes of Depression," All About Depression, 2013. allaboutdepression.com/cau_02.html.

15. Ree Hines, "Kristen Bell Reveals Why She Opened Up About Her Depression," *Today*, September 12, 2016. www.today.com/health/kristen-bell-reveals-why-she-opened-about-her-depression-t102755.

16. Stacey Freedenthal, Ph.D., LCSW, "Is a Suicide Attempt a Cry for Help?," Speaking of Suicide, 2013. www.speakingofsuicide.com/2013/06/17/cry-for-help/.

17. Jenny Lawson, "Wouldn't It Be Awesome to Just Have to Be Aware of Mental Health One Month a Year?," *The Bloggess*, May 29, 2015. thebloggess.com/2015/05/29/wouldnt-it-be-awesome-to-just-be-aware-of-mental-health-one-month-a-year/.

18. Anne-Sophie Bine, "Social Media Is Redefining 'Depression,'" *The Atlantic*, October 28, 2013. www.theatlantic.com/health/archive/2013/10/social-media-is-redefining-depression/280818/.

19. Quoted in Bine, "Social Media Is Redefining 'Depression.'"

20. Bine, "Social Media Is Redefining 'Depression.'"

Chapter Three: Treating Depression

21. Linda, interview by Lydia Bjornlund, May 14, 2009.

22. "Treating Premenstrual Dysphoric Disorder," *Harvard Health Publications*, October 2009. www.health.harvard.edu/womens-health/treating-premenstrual-dysphoric-disorder.

23. Chris Weller, "Antidepressants Aren't Taken by the Depressed; Majority of Users Have No Disorder," *Medical Daily*, April 2, 2015. www.medicaldaily.com/antidepressants-arent-taken-depressed-majority-users-have-no-disorder-327940.

24. "Interpersonal Therapy for Depression," WebMD, February 8, 2017. www.webmd.com/depression/guide/interpersonal-therapy-for-depression#1.

25. "ECT, TMS and Other Brain Stimulation Therapies," National Alliance on Mental

Illness. www.nami.org/Learn-More/Treatment/ECT,-TMS-and-Other-Brain-Stimulation-Therapies.

26. Julie K. Hersh, "The Shocking Truth about ECT," *Psychology Today*, April 24, 2015. www.psychologytoday.com/blog/struck-living/201504/the-shocking-truth-about-ect.
27. Anne Shea, e-mail interview by author, March 4, 2017.

Chapter Four: Taking Control of Depression

28. ScribusMedicus, "How Antidepressants Have Helped Me and My Family," Helium. www.helium.com/items/610203-how-antidepressants-have-helped-me-and-my-family.
29. Wiley Reading, "5 Things to Do (and Not Do) to Support Someone with Depression," *Everyday Feminism*, March 21, 2015. everydayfeminism.com/2015/03/supporting-people-with-depression/.
30. Anna Borges, "10 Tips for Talking to Your Parents About Your Mental Health," BuzzFeed, July 2, 2016. www.buzzfeed.com/annaborges/how-do-i-tell-my-parents-i-need-mental-health-help?utm_term=.pirG04z2L#.kuy3gVDyd.
31. Quoted in Depression-Guide.com, "What People Are Saying About Depression-Guide.com." www.depression-guide.com/index.htm.

Chapter Five: Learning More about Depression

32. Lindsay Abrams, "Study: Most People Diagnosed with Depression Do Not Actually Meet Criteria," *The Atlantic*, May 1, 2013.

www.theatlantic.com/health/archive/2013/05/study-most-people-diagnosed-with-depression-do-not-actually-meet-criteria/275436/.

33. Quoted in Shankar Vedantam, "Criteria for Depression Are Too Broad, Researchers Say," *Washington Post*, April 3, 2007. www.washingtonpost.com/wp-dyn/content/article/2007/04/02/AR2007040201693.html.
34. "What Causes Depression?," *Harvard Health Publications*, June 2009. www.health.harvard.edu/mind-and-mood/what-causes-depression.
35. "What Causes Depression?," *Harvard Health Publications*.
36. Quoted in Dan Harris, "A New Treatment for Depression: Magnets," ABC News, May 17, 2005. abcnews.go.com/WNT/Depression/Story?id=765933&page=1.
37. "ECT, TMS and Other Brain Stimulation Therapies," National Alliance on Mental Illness.
38. "Ketamine Lifts Depression via a Byproduct of its Metabolism," National Institute of Mental Health, May 4, 2016. www.nimh.nih.gov/news/science-news/2016/ketamine-lifts-depression-via-a-byproduct-of-its-metabolism.shtml.

GLOSSARY

antidepressants: Prescription medications that may be used to help treat depression.

anxiety: A state of heightened worry, uneasiness, or apprehension. Also a term for a group of mental disorders in which severe anxiety is a major symptom.

bipolar disorder: A disorder involving periods of extreme delight and energy highs countered with extreme sadness and hopelessness, often with periods of normal feelings between these extremes.

chronic: Long-lasting; always present or occurring over and over.

deoxyribonucleic acid (DNA): A substance that carries genetic information in the cells of plants and animals.

dysthymia: Also called dysthymic disorder, a type of depression characterized by moods that are consistently low over a long period of time.

genetic: Inherited from parents, the passing on of physical and behavioral traits.

hormone: A chemical produced by the endocrine system which regulates body processes such as growth, sleep, and digestion.

magnetic resonance imaging (MRI): A scan producing an image of the brain or other body part by mapping magnetic fields.

major depressive disorder: Also known as clinical depression, this mood disorder is characterized by feelings of intense sadness, irritability, changes in appetite and sleep, low self-esteem or self-worth, and feelings of hopelessness and despair.

neurotransmitter: A molecule responsible for transmission of a nerve impulse across the synapse between two nerve cells.

placebo: A medicine that generally has no effect on a disease and is prescribed by a doctor for the mental relief it offers a patient.

postpartum depression: A type of depression affecting some women who have recently given birth.

psychiatrist: A medical doctor with training in the diagnosis and treatment of mental and emotional illnesses.

psychologist: A professional who studies behavior and experience and who is licensed to provide therapeutic services.

psychotic depression: A disorder when a severe depressive illness is accompanied by some form of psychosis, such as hearing voices or having delusions or hallucinations.

seasonal affective disorder (SAD): A type of depression characterized by the onset of a depressive illness during the winter months, when there is less sunlight.

selective serotonin reuptake inhibitors (SSRIs): A class of antidepressant medication that helps the body use serotonin more effectively.

therapy: A form of treatment in which a psychiatrist, psychologist, or counselor works to help resolve a patient's mental or emotional issues.

trauma: Injury or stress caused by an outside force that may have long-lasting psychological effects.

ORGANIZATIONS TO CONTACT

American Psychiatric Association
1000 Wilson Blvd., Suite 1825
Arlington, VA 22209
(703) 907-7300
apa@psych.org
www.psychiatry.org
The American Psychiatric Association is a membership organization for psychiatrists and other physicians who are working to ensure effective diagnosis and treatment for people with mental disorders, including depression. The organization engages in a wide range of research and education activities.

American Psychological Association (APA)
750 First St. NE
Washington, DC 20002
(800) 374-2721
www.apa.org
The APA is a scientific and professional organization that represents psychologists in the United States. Its mission is to advance the creation, communication, and application of psychological knowledge to benefit society and improve people's lives.

Depression and Bipolar Support Alliance (DBSA)
55 E. Jackson Blvd., Suite 490
Chicago, IL 60604
(800) 826-3632
www.dbsalliance.org
Founded in 1985, the DBSA is a patient-directed national nonprofit organization that conducts research on mood disorders, provides support for sufferers and their families, educates the public, and lobbies on behalf of people living with mood disorders. The DBSA has a

grassroots network of patient-run support groups across the country.

Families for Depression Awareness
391 Totten Pond Rd., Suite 101
Waltham, MA 02451
(781) 890-0220
www.familyaware.org
Families for Depression Awareness is a national nonprofit organization that helps families and friends recognize and cope with depressive disorders to help people get well and prevent suicides. The organization provides education, outreach, and advocacy to support families. Families for Depression Awareness is made up of families who have lost a family member to suicide or have watched a loved one suffer with depression.

National Suicide Prevention Lifeline
(800) 273-8255
suicidepreventionlifeline.org
Sometimes people with depression find life so difficult that they think about suicide. The hotline and website, which includes a free online chat service, provide emotional support to people who are in a difficult time in their life.

FOR MORE INFORMATION

Books

Allen, Jon. *Coping with Depression: From Catch-22 to Hope*. Washington, DC: American Psychiatric Publishing, 2005.
This book addresses the challenges patients who are depressed face on the road to recovery, focusing particular attention on the importance of hope.

Brees, Karen K. *The Everything Health Guide to Depression: Reassuring Advice to Help You Feel Like Yourself Again*. Avon, MA: Adams Media, 2008.
This comprehensive book provides information about research into depression's symptoms, causes, and treatment.

Brosh, Allie. *Hyperbole and a Half: Unfortunate Situations, Flawed Coping Mechanisms, Mayhem, and Other Things That Happened*. London, UK: Square Peg, 2013.
Brosh alternates chapters containing funny stories about her childhood and her dogs with chapters that discuss how depression has affected her life and how she dealt with it.

Copeland, Mary Ellen, and Stuart Copans. *Recovering from Depression: A Workbook for Teens*. Baltimore, MD: Paul H. Brookes Publishing Co., 2002.
This workbook includes exercises to help young adults recognize the signs of depression in themselves, deal with their negative emotions in healthy ways, and reach out to friends and family for support.

Meisel, Abigail. *Depression and Bipolar Disorder: Examining Chemical Imbalances and Mood Disorders*. Berkeley Heights, NJ: Jasmine Health, 2015.
This book provides an in-depth look at bipolar disorder and depression, including causes and treatment options.

Websites

Mental Health America
www.nmha.org
Mental Health America is a nonprofit organization dedicated to helping people live mentally healthier lives. The organization seeks to promote mental wellness by educating the public; fighting for access to effective care; fostering innovation in research, practice, services, and policy; and providing support to individuals and families living with mental health and substance abuse problems. The website includes an informational screening test people can take to see whether they may be experiencing depression.

The Mighty
themighty.com
This website features stories by real people who are struggling with different kinds of mental and physical illnesses.

National Alliance on Mental Illness (NAMI)
www.nami.org
NAMI is a grassroots mental health advocacy organization. Since it began in 1979, NAMI has engaged in a wide range of support, awareness, education, advocacy, and research programs to improve the lives of individuals and families affected by mental illness.

National Institute of Mental Health (NIMH)
www.nimh.nih.gov
The mission of NIMH, which is part of the National Institutes of Health, is to transform the understanding and treatment of mental illnesses through basic and clinical research, paving the way for prevention, recovery, and cure. The organization offers research on and information about diagnosis, causes, and treatment of depression.

***Psychology Today* Therapist Finder**
therapists.psychologytoday.com/rms
Entering a zip code on this website gives a list of some therapists in the area. Each therapist's entry includes a short biography, a list of the issues they specialize in, the average cost per session, and any insurance plans that are accepted.

INDEX

C

D

E

F

N

P

R

S

T

U

W

Y

PHOTO CREDITS

Cover Monkey Business Images/Shutterstock.com; cover, back cover, 1–6, 10, 13, 22–23, 32–33, 44, 46–47, 53, 64, 69, 71, 75, 77, 80, 82, 86, 91, 93, 95, 97, 103, 104 (texture) foxaon1987/Shutterstock.com; p. 7 Marcos Mesa Sam Wordly/Shutterstock.com; pp. 8–9 SORANAT7/Shutterstock.com; p. 11 Antonio Guillem/Shutterstock.com; p. 14 polkadot_photo/Shutterstock.com; p. 17 Marjan Apostolovic/Shutterstock.com; p. 19 OndroM/Shutterstock.com; p. 23 Alex Malikov/Shutterstock.com; p. 25 OcusFocus/iStock/Thinkstock; p. 29 Donna Cuic/Shutterstock.com; p. 34 Designua/Shutterstock.com; p. 38 Featureflash Photo Agency/Shutterstock.com; p. 41 ZUMA Press Inc/Alamy Stock Photo; p. 43 Chepko Danil Vitalevich/Shutterstock.com; p. 48 A and N photography/Shutterstock.com; p. 50 megaflopp/Shutterstock.com; p. 52 Steve Cukrov/Shutterstock.com; p. 55 KatarzynaBialasiewicz/iStock/Thinkstock; p. 58 JACOPIN/BSIP/Superstock.com; p. 59 ©iStockphoto.com/Rocky89; p. 60 taa22/Shutterstock.com; p. 62 ESB Professional/Shutterstock.com; p. 66 kissenbo/iStock/Thinkstock; p. 69 Shvaygert Ekaterina/Shutterstock.com; p. 73 Lopolo/Shutterstock.com; p. 74 wavebreakmedia/Shutterstock.com; p. 76 JulijaDmitrijeva/iStock/Thinkstock; p. 79 Levent Konuk/Shutterstock.com; p. 81 adike/Shutterstock.com; p. 84 BSIP/UIG/Getty Images.

ABOUT THE AUTHOR

Simon Pierce grew up in Jamestown, New York. He later moved to New York City and completed his education at NYU. He now lives in Brooklyn with his partner and their son. He has written for various health and wellness publications over the past seven years. He and his family enjoy people-watching in the park or reading the names on cemetery headstones and inventing stories about them.